WINNING

WINNING

MOTIVATION FOR
BUSINESS, SPORT & LIFE

FRANK DICK O.B.E.

ABINGDON PUBLISHING

First published in Great Britain 1992
The Abingdon Management Company Ltd trading as Abingdon
Publishing, 22 Suffolk Street, London SW1Y 4HS

Reprinted 1997

A CIP catalogue record for this book is available from the British
Library

ISBN 1 872317 01 4

Edited and typeset by Davies & Dimant, Cambridge
Cover design by Garner Russell, 1 Wardour Mews,
London W1V 3FF
Photoset by Type & Style, 14-16 Dorland House, Regent Street,
London SW1Y 4PH
Printed and bound by Ennisfield Print & Design, Telfords Yard,
6-8 The Highway, Wapping,.
London E1 9BQ

ACKNOWLEDGEMENTS

I'd like to thank everyone who gave me reason to write and something to write about. What's written I've learned from those I've worked for and those I've worked with; from those I've taught or trained and those who've taught and trained me; from those in my own sport of athletics, from sport in general, from business and from education; and finally, from the friends and family I'm so privileged to have.

Especially, I'd like to thank some friends who created the climate which allowed the book to grow in my mind: Dr Hans Muller Wohlfahrt, Alan Finlay, Harry Wilson, Ion Tiriac, Daley Thompson, Andy Roxburgh, Dave Bedford, Andy Parker and Peter Witt.

Finally, I thank Geoffrey Hamilton-Fairley for believing in me enough to nudge me into writing it; Peter Davies for an incredible editing job; and Jackie Brown for being able to read my writing better than me.

I've had such really great times climbing mountains and tripping over molehills with all these people.

To Mum and Dad,
who gave me roots to grow,
and Linda,
who gave me wings to fly.

CONTENTS

Introduction: Warm Up   1

Chapter One: The Game   5

Chapter Two: The Athlete   21

Chapter Three: The Team   47

Chapter Four: The Coach   67

Chapter Five: The Personal Preparation Plan   99

Chapter Six: Taking the Lead   153

Chapter Seven: The Badge   181

Conclusion: Warm Down   197

WARM UP

There are two kinds of people in my world, valley people and mountain people.

Valley people seek the calm and comfortable ground of shelter, safety and security. They may talk about change, but do not want to be involved in it, especially if this means breaking from the routine of what's worked okay up till now. Their concept of achievement is 'not losing', so playing for the draw to them is all that's needed. Their concept of fitness, is being fit to survive. They are the people you meet whose sentences start with, 'I would have… ', 'I could have… ', or 'I should have… ' They are the almost people who have many explanations for not making it themselves and only one for those who have – luck. They talk about the risk of losing and yet, they are losers – they just don't know it.

Mountain people have decided that valley life is not for them, and seek to test ambition on the toughest climbs. They know that there is a rich satisfaction in reaching the top and the fight that's needed to get there. They live for the test of change and enjoy the resilience required to bounce back from the bumps and bruises that come with the mountain territory. They not only talk about change, they deliver it.

They take the risk of winning because, to them,

there's no such thing as a risk of losing. People can lose without training or practice, it comes quite naturally, so where's the risk in that? They know that achievement is not always reflected in a gold medal, but is always measured by the excitement of knowing just how much further their best shot takes them when they take the risk of winning.

Achievement is balanced on the finest of edges, but they know that, whatever the outcome of the contest, they are always accountable for the result. They are winners, and they know it.

I write this book for mountain people – people like you. It is about people who succeed, who achieve, who win – and who intend continuing to do so.

Each of us has mountains to climb. They may not all be Mount Everest but they're still our mountains. They can arise in our family and social life, in our business life, and in our personal life. You know what yours are, and you apply those qualities described in chapter two, *The Athlete*, to get to the top of each.

But personal abilities and commitment can often be used to even greater effect when people work together as a team. *The Team*, chapter three, builds on *The Athlete* to bring into perspective the idea that 'the whole is greater than the sum of the parts'.

Neither athlete nor team will make progress, however, without *Preparation Planning* under the thoughtful guidance of *The Coach*. These chapters look more closely at how to take on even bigger mountains. In particular, they focus on the need for understanding and applying a coaching style of management in pursuit of achievement, and in the development of essential skills when *Taking the Lead*.

I believe that there are many situations in life where we are required to be coaches, team members, and athletes. Only with this kind of adaptability and creativity can we develop and maintain the values embraced by our culture – what we fight for – our *Badge*.

This brings me to the mountains themselves. The slopes to be conquered, the game to be won, is change: creating it, managing it, staying in control of it. This is the subject of chapter one, *The Game*. I believe that the game is there to be won – and that it's for you to do the winning.

CHAPTER ONE
THE GAME

It is a fact of life that we are all competitive and that the most competitive games attract the most competitive people. They know that the purpose of competing in these games is to go for the win, to achieve their objectives. They do so individually or as a member of a team, by giving their best shot in the competitive arena of the game they choose to play. From the moment the game starts until it's over, they pursue the objectives they've carefully prepared to meet. They play within the rules and do not try to stretch them. They always win whatever the final score. You are one of these people.

Without doubt, the toughest of all games is change. Some people would say that it is the only game. Change, then, is the game that must be won. The truth is, that in everything we do, be it in our personal, family, social or business lives, whatever our talents and skills, there is a constant need to be in control of change and its effects. It's your capacity to have and to maintain this control which determines whether or not you are an achiever.

In sport, it is the coach's job to help athletes develop that control, and to ensure that they are afforded the sort of supportive environment they need to remain in control. This is the most sophisticated area of the coach's art. It makes more certain that the basic building blocks of technique, tactics and training are rewarded by the level of achievement that the athlete's talent and commitment deserve. It is also the coach's job to develop this control of change in himself or herself. Winning athletes are always trained by winning coaches.

The trouble with discussing 'change' is that it can sound too abstract. You need something you can bite on. I'll try and explain my thoughts on the matter by looking at, and reflecting on, personal experience of situations in competitive sport, in business and in life in general.

I believe there are four aspects to the game of change:

1. A commitment to change is a lifetime commitment.
2. Every game contains both fixed and flexible parts.
3. Players can either impose change or be exposed to it.
4. Preparation will help you win this game.

Commitment to change

The 1980 Olympic Games 100 metres in Moscow was won by Allan Wells (GBR) in 10.25 seconds. Last place in the 100 metres final at the 1990 World Championships in Tokyo was Bruny Surin (Canada) in 10.14 seconds. Carl Lewis (USA) won the 1988 Seoul Olympics 100 metres final in the world record time of 9.92 seconds. Three years later, Linford Christie (GBR) equalled that time yet finished fourth in the Tokyo World Championships. I hope I've made my point. Human physical performance goes on improving at an amazing pace. And there's not the slightest chance of such improvement slowing down within our lifetime – nor even in that of our grandchildren. If anything we are likely to see the pace of change accelerate. As Alvin Toffler points out in his book *Future Shock*, the world today is as different from that into which our fathers were born, as that world was from Julius Caesar's. And he wrote that in 1970 – how much further and faster have we moved since then?

Change is inevitable. In the words of Robert Burns, 'Look abroad through nature's range, nature's mighty law is change.' You might as well try to stop the world and get off as try to halt change. Far better to accept it, welcome it, even influence it. Afterall, in a changing world, change is the only thing you can really count on and change is on your side. Everything from changes in society and our capacity to work together, to the new technology that's left us free to do what we're best at – being creative, and getting on with the job – is in favour of our continuing improvement of personal performance. This is what Ron Dennis, the chief executive of the McLaren Formula One team, was getting at when he introduced his new 'fly-by-wire' car with its semi-automatic gearbox and cableless throttle: 'My aim is to have no connection between the driver and the engine. That way the driver is just free to drive, like a fighter pilot is free to fight. Nothing else must cloud his judgement, and his margin for making mistakes must be reduced to a minimum.'

Athletics shows us that we are well short of reaching the limit of our potential in physical performance. But just think how much our personal total performance will continue to improve as abilities and skills go on expanding and our capacity to use them expands too. We can and will equip ourselves to achieve targets and objectives which even a year ago would have seemed impossible. It's by accepting that change is a constant in our lives and by believing that we can adapt to it and use it to our advantage that we can respond to Babe Ruth's, 'Yesterday's home runs don't win tomorrow's ball games', with the desire, belief and persistence to score the home runs needed to win in tomorrow's games.

Playing to win in this game of change, then, means you never stop, because change never stops. You must learn to live life on the move. It's as if you've decided to board a spaceship heading out on a voyage of discovery, rather then board a merry-go-round heading round in unchanging circles. With every change comes expectation of more change and the need to adjust our focus for the future. That means not only in how we do things, but in how we think. No performance or result can be seen as final, but rather as a stage in achievement.

I'd like you to be predictable in that you'll always go for the win in this game, yet unpredictable in how you'll do it.

*Winning isn't everything,
it's the only thing.*

*Defeat is worse than death.
You have to live with defeat.*

Bill Shankley
(page 26)

The fixed and the flexible

The fixed things in this game you can't change. They represent the framework within which you will operate – your points of reference. The flexible things you can change. They represent how you operate to win. The fixed things, like the rules of a game or the law of the land must be assessed, adapted to and applied to the limit for this year's competition. The rules and laws may, of course, have changed from those which applied last year or even last competition, but you cannot change them at *this* point. You can only change how you'll play within the framework of rules which you must not only uphold, but defend. We are, in many ways, their guardians.

Perhaps the most important fixed element of all, and the one we must defend most of all, are our own values. These are the one aspect of a person that is fixed. They represent the person's 'real self' under all the wrapping of projected image, corporate persona and so on. Mark McCormack put it this way: 'The real self – one's true nature – can't change colour to suit its environment.' It is important to hold on to this 'real self' especially in moments of extreme change when it gives you a fixed point by which to navigate the new uncharted territory. I believe that it is essential to understand who the 'real self' is in each of the athletes I work with, otherwise I can neither develop nor deal with them. This is the person I am coaching towards achievement. This is the person who must learn to create and control the changes he or she must pursue to be a winner, sometimes despite that fixed 'self', but always through it.

The flexible things, like those relating to the opposition, to the athletes in your team, or to the specifics of a given competition, you must first assess or even create. Then you must develop and learn how to manage and control them to your advantage whether this is on a day-to-day basis or at the crisis level of minute-to-minute. In general terms, the most flexible pieces in the game are to do with people – you, the people on your team and, of course, the people on the opposition's team. They include, in sport, athletes, coaches and all support people, and in business, all staff, management and customers. They are most readily changed by their own desires and decisions, by the influence and actions of others, and by their response to the constraints of the fixed aspects of the game.

It's not always easy to differentiate between the fixed and the flexible, especially when you are in the arena and absorbed by the struggle of the competition. The trick, I believe, is to see the points on the score board as 'fixed'. There's nothing you can do about them. Whether they're yours or the opposition's they're gone – they're history. But there are a lot of points left in the game we're playing and again in tomorrow's games. They are still flexible and there's a lot you can do about them. They are the future and they're there to be won.

One of the greatest success stories in business in the early 1990's belongs to a company who dealt most effectively with the fixed and the flexible. The strength of tradition in an industry is the image of enduring quality. The weakness is that it may encourage complacency. Cadbury Limited, carries rich traditions going back to the 1860's yet management had the courage through the 'Cadbury means quality' initiative to prepare its people to accelerate the business through a process of change that catapulted the company towards the twenty first century. Cadbury Limited and its values are fixed. The Cadbury's people and their commitment are flexible.

Imposing change and being exposed to it

There is nothing more difficult to take in hand, more perilous to conduct, or more uncertain in its success, than to take the lead in the introduction of a new order of things. Because the innovator has for enemies all those who have done well under the old conditions and only lukewarm defenders in the those who may do well under the new.

Machiavelli

In every arena you are either imposing change or being exposed to it. If you are imposing change on your own team, you must make sure they are prepared for it and you must take time to coach them through it. The England rugby team changed tactics in the 1991 World Cup final. The players had not been prepared for such a change especially under the particular pressures of the final. They lost. If you are imposing change on the opposition, the edge you are seeking rests mainly on the opposition not being prepared for it. This was the purpose of the tactic used by the British 4 x 400 metres relay team at the 1991 World Championships in Tokyo in running Roger Black, our fastest 400 metres runner, first. The USA team had never experienced pressure on all four legs of the relay in previous major championships and we hoped the pressure we could place on them right from the start might cause them to lose their concentration. It did. The British team won.

Because you know before you get into the arena that everything from the opposition to the weather will expose you to change you must be prepared to adjust the details of your game-plan quickly and correctly to turn each situation to your advantage. You use each point won to fuel the motivation tank for more. You use each point lost to fuel the same tank and come back even harder than before. Daley Thompson had a disaster of a high jump in the 1986 European Championship decathlon in Stuttgart. We walked to the warm-up track with only the 400 metres left on the first day. 'Frankie, that was the most stupid thing I've ever done... ' was how he put it. Then he stopped me in my stride and with his finger only an inch from my nose said, 'You think you've seen great 400 metres before; today, you'll see the greatest.' He ran 47.02 seconds, only 0.16 seconds short of his lifetime best for 400 metres in a very windy stadium. It was, indeed, the best I'd seen.

The situation in the arena is constantly changing. Each change is something that you must have control of. When you change how you play, it must be to take control, to impose change on the opposition. If you don't, they see it as weakness, as grasping at a straw and it makes, rather than breaks, their motivation.

In the Tokyo World Championships women's 10,000 metres in 1991 Liz McColgan (GBR) was churning out lap after lap of relentless pace. The opposition, all world class, were buckling under the onslaught, except for one, Derartu Tulu (Ethiopia). She had been within two or three metres throughout, until lap seventeen, with only eight laps remaining, when she changed from following to leading. If she was going to take control in passing McColgan she would have to inject a new level of pace, throwing down a new gauntlet. But she didn't, she simply settled to the same pace. By not lifting the pace to put pressure on McColgan, Tulu was signalling, 'I'm not able to control this race.' McColgan received the message clearly and overtook again, accelerating away from Tulu and pressed on to win the gold medal.

When people change to simply contain a situation, they're in the survival business, not the winning business. It has become a damage limitation exercise where they hope the situation will burn itself out or the full-time whistle will blow early. Tulu's was not a challenge but a desperate gesture to try and contain McColgan. When people change they should do so to take control – then they're in the winning business.

*Exercise will not put years
on your life, but it will put life
in your years.*

Per-Olaf Asrand
(page 113)

Preparing to win

We're all probably exposed to change most often by our team leaders, our captains and our managers. Yet, they may fall short of preparing us properly for it. Such change is, without doubt, aimed at making us perform better individually and as a team, yet if you're not careful, the response can be anything from inconvenience and discomfort to fear and resentment, even resistance.

Whether creating change and imposing it, or being exposed to change and managing it, I think that there is a problem only when there is failure to ensure that people are properly prepared for the situation, and coached through it. When there's no preparation or coaching, change first makes people uncomfortable, because what could be dealt with routinely yesterday requires a new response today. That requires concentration of thought and effort, so for some there will be a feeling that they can't cope and that the leadership has opened a credibility gap. In short, there is a loss of confidence. Next, change is seen as a threat, because although the people measured up well to meeting yesterday's familiar challenge and to applying yesterday's familiar methods, they might not be up to today's. Now, there is a loss of trust. Finally, change defeats them because they lack the skills and attitude to deal with it, they are exhausted by the extra energy demands and emotional stress, and in a rising pool of self-doubt and disillusionment, they lose heart.

It is vital to recognise that such a range of responses is possible. Only then will we begin to look for ways to make people excited and enthusiastic about change; not only to accept that they are playing a game of change, but to want to win it.

I believe the solution is simple, but it has to be worked at really hard and continuously by everyone involved. How many times do you come across organisations which first decide that changes will be made, then tell people in the organisation with a fanfare of trumpets and roll of drums at an 'event' why changes have to be made and what these changes are, then do very little thereafter to help people through the traumatic process of making these changes? I can't ever imagine coaching an athlete or team to change techniques or tactics in such a way. Not only would it be unfair to the athlete, it would also be a recipe for failure. Instead, we would work at it over and over again until the changes were established in thought and in action so that they could be applied in the toughest and most varied of competitive environments.

So what is the simple solution? The way I see it is that you cannot achieve in a world of change by accident. You have to plan for it to make it happen. This is what leads me to believe we should adopt a *coaching style of management* for preparing people to win the game of change.

In coaching athletes, I first look at what the competition is going to be like four years ahead to determine what it is they are being prepared for. In fact, I try to look wider than the specific target to work out what life in general will be like by then. Then, a rough plan is drawn up to prepare them to reach that destination. It's a plan that will be delivered by working with the athlete to meet its demands. The coach develops the athlete through the plan. The detail of the plan, however, must be capable of adjustment at any time in the course of the 'journey'. Because the programme is always projected four years ahead, the destination is never a terminus. Finally, a very simple philosophy is applied in practice: 'Life by the yard is apt to be hard; life by the inch is a bit of a cinch.' Here I look at specific targets for the athlete a few weeks ahead, a few months ahead or a season ahead. These all lead up to the goal we want to achieve in four years, but in the meantime give the athlete a sense of day-to-day achievement.

After the Seoul Olympics in 1988, I was sitting on a plane with Dalton Grant, the British high jumper, going through what it would take to get a medal in the Barcelona Olympics of 1992. In 1988 Dalton had reached two metres 31 centimetres, but I estimated he would need to jump two metres 40 centimetres for a medal next time around. 'Great,' came the response, 'that's only two centimetres a year and an extra centimetre in the final!'

The whole point of preparing people to win in this game is to equip them to use the opportunities that change represents. Our game will be won by adopting this approach to preparing ourselves and our people and by sticking to it, whether points are won or lost as we develop the necessary skills. We create the chance of the win by going for the next point every time. We do so by catching the opposition out of position, or by putting the opposition into a position where his or her options are closed down to those which put you in with a winning chance. We aim at the same time to get into a position where our strengths can be used and the opposition can't use theirs. Making the chances, moving into position for a shot, passing the ball to another player better positioned to use it to the advantage of the team, seeing problems as opportunities waiting to be grasped – *this* is how we must individually and collectively play the game.

I believe that you are already well into preparation – otherwise you would not even open a book like this. You understand golfer Gary Player's point when he says, 'The harder I practice and work at my game, the luckier I get.' The idea now is to help you compete with even greater success, and to help those who have problems in playing this game achieve the success that you and I would wish them to have.

It won't be easy, because the competition is getting tougher by the day. The whole world is changing faster and faster and we've got to be in control to call the shots as it happens. We've moved from a world that was industry controlled to one that's information centred, from knowing the answer to knowing how and where to get it. We've moved from having to react to situations, to anticipating them or responding constructively to turn each of them to our advantage. Learning and preparing to create and manage change takes time, but in the end you are in control. And that's the only place to be for a winner.

CHAPTER TWO

THE ATHLETE

Where do winners come from?

I've given this question quite a bit of thought. Some people can't even seem to see the point of it. For them winning athletes do not come *from* anywhere. They're not formed by any process, they simply are. They put their faith in talent and for them building a strong team is simply a case of talent spotting. Pick the best people, stand back and watch them perform.

I've met loads of people who hold this view – athletes, commentators, and selectors among them – but not once have I heard it from a coach. I have been lucky enough to work with very gifted individuals every day of my working life and have the healthiest respect for their talent, but I know it has never done my job for me, or theirs for them. To spot a winning athlete, I am convinced you must look first and foremost for athletes with the passion to achieve, the desire to be the best in their chosen arena. If an athlete is a genius in the high jump but is actually in love with basketball – the probability is that basketball will be his best arena. Talent always comes a poor second to this kind of passion.

I first really understood about where talent stood in the scale of things when I discovered what I thought at the time was a unique problem. The National Schools

Athletics Championships in England produces outstanding champions every year. However, in the late 1970's it was commonplace for us to lose up to three quarters of these champions within a couple of years. No one can afford to lose high quality people at such a rate and the mystery preyed on my mind. In the end I mentioned the problem to a friend, Miroslav Vanek, who at that time was President of the International Federation of Sport Psychologists. I didn't expect him to have an answer, but I thought he might be interested in such an unusual problem.

'What makes you think that this situation is the prerogative of the capitalist west?' he asked in surprise. 'We have exactly the same problems in Czechoslovakia. It's like this. Your young champions are so because they are talented. They're not yet long enough into the discipline of training to be reaping its benefits so it's clear they are more talented than those who are seconds, thirds and fourths. On the other hand, those athletes have a different kind of motivation. In particular, although they win more often than they lose, they lose more often than the champions. This makes for a valuable learning experience. Coaches can use it to help the athletes develop a resilience to defeat and this is something more than talent alone can do.' Miroslav went on to plot a graph of motivation against talent something like this:

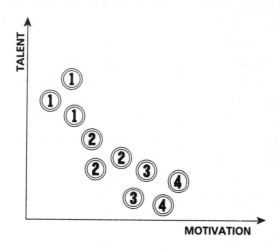

The numbers represented athletes' placings in competitions – first, second, third and fourth. Each of them had a unique profile of motivation and talent. It was evident that the most talented athletes did not have the same high level of motivation as the less gifted who had had to learn to deal with defeat. The question was, who was best prepared for the tougher world of senior sport? Clearly not the athletes who had developed the expectation of an arena which offered them little challenge. These athletes had not had the chance to develop a resilience to defeat – a resilience they would need in the senior arena where every athlete, no matter how able, sooner or later faces defeat. Because their abilities had never been challenged, these athletes had never stretched themselves. They had never had to change or to respond to change and while they were winners they had not been playing a game of change. The less talented athletes had been obliged to learn, to adapt, to fight, to bounce back. They had learnt to face change.

Suddenly, it is no longer a case of just talent spotting, but also motivation spotting. Talent alone simply isn't enough to get to the top. It comes down to establishing and developing the right profile of talent and motivation. We might not all be able to alter the natural talents we're given but athletes and coaches can create and manage a motivational climate in which we can achieve anything.

In this respect what really separates the achievers from the 'almost' people – the mountain people from the valley people – is mostly what goes on behind the eyes. The winning edge lies here. It is a state of mind, a philosophy if you like, but a simple one. In general, achievers need only three qualities – what I call **winners' life-skills** – to create their motivational climate.

1. You must want to win enough.
2. You must believe you can win.
3. You must persist until you do win.

Wanting

I believe that we all want to win when faced by a challenge. Indeed, this is really part of seeing something as a challenge. Goodness knows how early this starts in life, but it's my guess that the desire to achieve an objective,

*The harder I practice and work at
my game, the luckier I get.*

Gary Player

(page 19)

to win, comes very early in life. You can see it in the eyes of your children. The problem is that we are often taught to see that impulse as childish and suppress it. Winners, however, are those for whom wanting to win is something that just can't be suppressed. For them it's almost a need and to follow it through to achievement requires something more than ambition. Scotland's first chief coach, Lady Macbeth, put it this way when doing her husband's performance appraisal: 'Thou art not without ambition, but without the sickness that should attend it.' For the winner, the impulse to drive towards achievement is as basic as the impulse to eat or drink.

Bill Shankley, the Liverpool manager, understood this better than most. In his words, 'Winning isn't everything, it's the only thing,' or again, 'Defeat is worse than death. You have to live with defeat.' Hard talking, indeed, but the kind of words that winners understand and the kind that have kept Liverpool a force in world football two decades after Shanks' retirement. Wanting to win is an appetite that can't be satisfied. It means wanting to keep on winning forever, whatever it takes (within the rules).

Ion Tiriac is now best known as Boris Becker's manager and as one of the most successful entrepreneurs in sport. He was formerly a world class tennis doubles player with Ilye Nastase but early life for him was not what he now enjoys. As a youngster he chose to try out for the Romanian ice hockey team. At his first training camp, in the Romanian mountains, Ion remembers the coach singling him out: 'You, Tiriac, do you see that mountain behind you? There's a shop at the top of it where they sell cigarettes. Go and get me a pack of twenty.' The words were hardly out of his mouth before the young Tiriac was scrambling up the grassy slopes, struggling through forests, climbing over rocks and boulders, towards the summit, up to his armpits in snow, eventually reaching the shop. He bought the cigarettes and ran back down the mountain, slipping, stumbling, falling but finally reaching the coach. Ion handed him the packet of cigarettes. 'No, Tiriac, not the cigarettes in the green packet, the ones in the red packet!' Ion says, 'I didn't wait to hear his next instruction. I took the packet from him and made sure my eyes were laughing as I looked into his. Then I ran even faster up the mountain. I wanted him to know my spirit could not be beaten. I wanted him to know I wanted to make that team and wouldn't stop running up and down that mountain till I made it.' Of course, he did.

Believing

Believing you can win is the next part of your mental armoury. Quite simply, if you don't believe you can win you won't! This really needs to be worked at and every top achiever I've come across does just that, working on their mental state as hard as on their physical conditioning. They believe they are winners.

I was coaching Daley Thompson in California in April 1986 and at the end of a long sun drenched day I had eased myself into a chair to watch the sunset at his house on Capistrano beach. It was nice there on the verandah. I was sipping a very cold beer as I watched a pelican fly low over the water on its way south towards San Diego. I wondered at the way the tired sun seemed to suddenly drop like a stone into the Pacific horizon. I listened to the dolphins splashing as they played close to the beach. 'What a tough life,' I thought. Daley appeared on the wall in front of me and out of nowhere asked me one of those questions I'd come to expect in a long line of our own version of Trivial Pursuit. 'Frankie, who's the greatest athlete you ever saw?' The names of great sportsmen and women sped through my mind, those I'd watched live and on TV. I admitted it was a hard question and began to go through what I considered to be my short list. Daley let me get to seven or eight names, then stopped me in my tracks with, 'Forget it, buddy, you're looking at him!'

You might call that arrogance – and certainly many winners have a 'rough edge' of arrogance – but it's the good side of arrogance. It's what Scots call 'having a guid conceit of yourself'. All that Daley was doing was reinforcing what I admit was a well deserved and well groomed belief in himself. Such rough edges are what make winners special and you smooth them down at the risk of making them the same as everyone else. We all know already that the last thing any of us needs to get the best out of ourselves is to be told we're the same as everyone else and to be treated the same as everyone else. Winners are first and foremost individuals, because winning singles you out.

Of the three qualities winners need there can be no doubt that belief is the most fragile. It can be knocked out of you very easily but by the same token it can be readily restored. Winning athletes and coaches are very aware of this and each constantly services the motivational climate required to keep self-belief sharp. No one should assume that it is always there.

Katarina Witt is the greatest female skater of all time. On the ice she radiates beauty, sophistication and, without doubt, confidence. Yet before the competition, she is as frightened as any great athlete. The competition, of course, represents an exciting opportunity to create a masterpiece of movement but when the gate closes, it is lonely out there on the ice. Her coach, Jutta Muller says the same thing before each competition and puts her hand on Katarina's to give more reassuring strength to her words, 'You have done it before, you will do it again.' She always does.

Persisting

In many people's minds, this is the most important of the three qualities. Calvin Coolidge put it like this:

'Nothing in the world can take the place of persistence. Talent will not, nothing is more common than unsuccessful men with talent. Genius will not, unrewarded genius is almost a proverb. Education will not, the world is full of educated derelicts. Persistence and determination alone are omnipotent.'

In 1989 at the AAA Championships in Birmingham,

Seb Coe was determined to make the England team in the 1500 metres for the 1990 Commonwealth Games in Auckland, New Zealand, but was equally determined to demonstrate that the BAAB Council was in error in failing to support the selectors' opinion that he should go to the 1988 Seoul Olympics. Four hundred and fifty metres from the finish, a clash of arms and legs produced a series of stumbles which almost had Seb out of the race. In fact, he lost ten metres to the leader. He then had the same sort of choice we all have from time to time. He could have walked off the track. Who would blame him? Only himself, because winners don't have walking away as a choice that's theirs. He could have got mad and sprinted to the front to reassert his influence on the opposition – only to risk running out of steam. But again, winners don't put uncontrolled emotions high on their list of choices. He could remember that the finishing line was still 450 metres away and that *this* was now the race that had to be won. He did that. He adapted to the change in that particular game and he won.

Persistence, determination, staying the course – this is what it finally takes to win. It is also this that has made me convinced that real winners win even when they lose.

In the 1991 Tokyo World Championships 100 metres final, Great Britain's Linford Christie ran 9.92 seconds, which equalled the 1988 Olympic Games winning time, a time which still stood as a world record in 1991. He finished fourth, but can this be considered failure? It was an outstanding achievement and surpassed the predic-

Some men see things as they really are and ask, 'why?'
I dream of things that never were and ask, 'why not?'

George Bernard Shaw
(page 43)

tions of almost every authority on what he was worth. Medals here simply were not the right criteria of measuring achievement. Linford was a winner in Tokyo.

I cannot understand those people who discourage pursuit of achievement. You know the sort of people I mean – permanent valley residents – who argue that since normally only one athlete wins in a competition lots of athletes will lose. Consequently they see competition as something that provides a high probability of athlete failure. Of course, you compete to win but if you don't, you fight for next best, or to give a better account of yourself than you've given previously, or at worst you walk away having learned a lot to help you next time. Competition, then, provides a high probability of athlete achievement. What's important is how we look at achievement.

Before the Rome World Athletics Championships in 1987, Daley Thompson had to work his way back from a pretty serious adductor strain. The adductors are the muscles you need to be able to bring your legs together. In the last days before the decathlon, although training performances were good, I still didn't feel comfortable for him, so I asked, 'Are you sure about this, chief?' 'Frankie, we agreed a long time ago, if you never try, you never know.' So he tried, but the winning edge was not there. After the pole vault on the second day, he came off and joked that I should buy two tickets for the Bahamas and that we should leave 'Now!' We tried to laugh and tried not to cry, but somehow communication between brain and emotions got confused. He said, 'You know, I'm only doing this to remind myself why I like winning.' Then, some minutes later, 'You don't know how unhappy I am.' He did the final event, the 1500 metres because he could justify the physical and emotional pain to himself if he could help a friend, Gary Kinder of the USA towards a personal record. When it was over, Andy Higgins the Canadian decathlon coach caught up with us in a tunnel under the stand. 'Daley this performance is better than your Olympic golds and world records. It's taken more of a man to do what you have just done than it took when everything was going your way.' He was right. Daley's real character had taken over. He was as much a winner stumbling and picking himself up as he was climbing the winner's rostrum all those times.

The way a man wins, shows much of his character.
The way he loses, shows all of it.

Canute Rockne

Daley's example is the clearest I've ever seen that no one is a part-time winner. A winner is a winner whether training or relaxing, in victory or in defeat. Winning is not a job that one works on nine to five and then puts aside. It becomes a way of life twenty-four hours a day for people who decide to be winners. This is what I call the professional approach to achievement. Professional is not the opposite of amateur. I know many athletes in amateur sport with a very professional attitude to achievement. It has little to do with money, but a great deal to do with attitude and strength of character. This carries right through winners' lives and in my opinion is often most clearly illustrated in their actions well away from their arena.

In 1989 at the Formula One Grand Prix race at Imola, Gerhard Berger hit a wall at 175mph. The car instantly burst into flames and the fuel tank exploded leaving the unconscious Berger in a ball of fire for the thirty seconds it took to extinguish the flames. It had been hot enough in there for his helmet to start to melt. His father and close family friend, Horst Roger, waited in the hospital casualty department. They were in a state of shock and did not know how bad the situation was. Berger was carried into the department and had only just begun to come around. He caught sight of the shocked pair – and winked. This tells you more about Gerhard Berger than any history of his racing achievements. His thought at that moment was to put two frightened minds at ease. Winners have an extraordinary capacity for separating out the important from the unimportant at any given moment and for dealing effectively and quickly with the important. (I must say, however, that this is the same guy who dressed me in a purple ski suit with gold and brown striped sleeves and a pair of ladies' pink ski boots, put me on extra long skis, and took me to the top of a mountain, knowing I couldn't ski, and then told me, 'Remember the pain you gave me in training this morning? Good. I'll see you at the bottom of the piste.')

Winning, then is a choice for life. If you decide it's for you, then you must reflect that decision in every aspect of your life. Three great authorities on the subject, separated by centuries and cultures summed it up this way:

The Athlete

We are or we become those things which we
repeatedly do. Therefore excellence can become not
just an event but a habit.

Albert Einstein

Winning is not a one time thing, it's an all the time thing.
You don't win once in a while; you don't do things right
once in a while. You do things right all the time.
Winning is a habit. Unfortunately, so is losing.

Vince Lombardi

Excellence is an art won by training and habituation.
We are what we repeatedly do. Excellence, then,
is not an act but a habit.

Aristotle

Wanting to win, believing you can win and persisting until you win are the three good habits that all winners pursue throughout their lives. They are the essential long term bases of any achievement. However, in the tight timescales of the competition itself, such deeply ingrained habits need to become instinctive. All winners must also work on those short-term skills that see them through in the arena itself when it comes to a one-on-one crisis. These are what I call the **arena skills** and they are the cutting edge of the winning habit.

I vividly remember watching Stefan Edberg trail Miroslav Mecir by two sets and love-four in their 1988 Wimbledon semi-final. It had been so one-sided many of Stefan's disappointed fans had left their seats rather than see their hero beaten. That was a pity. He fought back and won both the semi-final and the final. This is just one among a series of incredible turnabouts I have seen in tennis and other sports over the years and the ability to take advantage of them has always been for me a hall-mark of the very finest sportsmen. I always used to wonder how such winners could recognise the chance when anyone else would have said they were dead and buried. Boris Becker's view is that you can see it in your opponent's eyes. What you see is far worse than fear because fear can be the shot of adrenalin the player needs; it's self doubt, it's losing control of your will, it's seeing a situation not as a 'bruise' but as a 'dislocation', it's feeling that it's you that's wrong and not your action. This is what happens if you stop believing you can win. Even in the most extreme situations, even against reason, you need to hold onto that with both hands. Whatever the situation, be it at the beginning, the middle or the end of the game, you can never let your opponent see in your eyes that he or she has beaten who you are.

The first arena skill, then, is **watchfulness**. However tired you are, it is vital to observe everything, to read the game. Seeing the moment might give you the chance to come back from the edge of defeat or to pick the right moment to strike and end the contest. Signals that present tactics are correct, that it's time to step up the pressure or continue to absorb it are meat and drink to winners. 'Watchfulness' means using all your senses and instincts to learn and get the edge. Don't rely on precon-ceived ideas and second-hand hunches. If you do you'll

Persistence, determination, staying the course – this is what it finally takes to win. It is also this that has made me convinced that real winners win even when they lose.

(page 30)

No one is a part-time winner. A winner is a winner whether training or relaxing, in victory or defeat.

(page 33)

miss the vital changes that are unique to this game. Open your senses to work out everything from your opponent's strengths to what he or she is not so happy with. This is part of the trade of winning. Winners do so by plying their trade. Losers must rely on the 'tricks of the trade' because they've never taken time to master it and know that you have. Just remember that old line, 'It's never over till it's over.'

One sure thing that will stop you watching for what you need to win will be if you lose your focus on the game before you. Winners remember what the game *is*, not what it *means*, all the time. **Focus** is the second arena skill. The game is no different be it a qualifying round or the final; be it the first point or the match point; whether you played the last point brilliantly or dreadfully. As Bill Shankley told his young players, 'Every time you touch the ball is the most important touch you'll have in the game.'

At the 1971 European Athletics Championships in Helsinki, the women's discus was a nail-biting battle between Lisl Westermann of the Federal Republic of Germany and Faina Melnik of the Soviet Union. Westermann held the world record and every throw in the first five rounds was ahead of Melnik. In the sixth and final round Westermann, throwing one place ahead of Melnik in the throwing order stretched her lead. The Finnish crowd went wild as they always take some pleasure in seeing their neighbour, the Russian 'Bear' beaten. Two markers located the European Championship and the world record on the grass which seemed even brighter green under the floodlights. Melnik walked into the circle and looked out over that bright green grass. The crowd went so silent you could hear the moths flitting in and out of the floodlights. Melnik crouched at the back of the circle, prepared to throw, spun and launched the discus. It passed her own best mark of the competition. It passed Westermann's new European Championship record. It passed Westermann's world record. It gave Melnik her first ever world record. It was just another throw, just another competition. She made her total statement.

Being watchful can also mean watching yourself and focusing on your own feelings. It's important to be aware of your own feelings, to remind yourself you're a winner if you begin to lose your belief. Equally, it's important to watch for over-confidence. There's a thin line between believing you can win and believing you can't lose. This is a really dangerous attitude, because here you have no respect for the opposition. Whatever arena you're in, the opposition is not going to roll onto its back, kick its legs in the air and say, 'Okay, you can win today!' No victory is worth having if the opposition isn't worth beating.

In the final match of the rugby international season in 1990, England went to face Scotland at Murrayfield, to play what most experts predicted would be a fairly straightforward affair. As one English tabloid put it, 'We'll go in like the SAS. We'll take no prisoners.' Any athlete who begins to believe such comment is in big trouble. Yet, to be honest it is difficult to ignore – it can get inside your head without being invited. My own advice to athletes is to avoid reading newspapers in the days leading up to a key competition. On the day, the England team ran onto the pitch effervescent in anticipation of the predicted outcome. They were thinking about the final whistle before the kick-off – a classic focus problem. The Scottish team walked onto the pitch with a grim determination etched onto their faces. They won. The same English tabloid on the Monday morning wrote, 'SAS? They were more like the WRVS!' I've often smiled at how 'we' on Friday became 'they' on Monday. You know, it's rough enough for athletes to be out there fighting, without having to be held accountable for the exasperations and frustrations of the critics.

Related to this is what I've come to recognise as the **qualifying flats**. It is this that catches champions unawares when they are eliminated or nearly eliminated in the early qualifying rounds of a competition. If they have their minds set on the final already, rather than focused on the game in hand, they may find it hard to 'get up' for the preliminary competitions. These 'nuisance value' rounds must, however, be won to get there. You don't jump from the top of one mountain to the top of the next. You have, once again, to deal with the foothills. It's not quite like serving your apprenticeship again. It's more like remembering that the championship is the whole competition not just part of it. Qualifying flats hit the very best if they are off-guard. What you have to bear in mind is that the opposition see achievement in the qualifying rounds as a matter of life

You have to get a feeling for the athlete's technique as a whole. If there is a problem, a little one or a big one, you'll spot it straight away because either the big picture looks right and has rhythm and balance, or it seems slightly out of focus, or it just isn't right at all. It's not possible to do this by standing too close. You have to stand back to get the big picture.

Anatolyi Bonderchuk,
(page 98)

and death, and you must still want to win every bit as badly as them. Tommy McKean, British 800 metres runner and favourite for a medal in the 1991 Tokyo World Championships went home after the first round. Wrexham humbled Arsenal in the third round of the FA Cup in 1992. Boris Becker lost in the third round of Wimbledon the year after winning the championship for the second time to the unknown Peter Doohan. Champions quickly learn that the early rounds are very tough rounds. They learn because the humiliation of such defeats is hard to forget.

Again, 'Yesterday's home runs don't win tomorrow's ball games', is the lesson here. By all means enjoy each achievement, but remember that it's over when it's over. The worst kind of hangover is the one suffered by winners who live on yesterday's triumphs. What it took to win yesterday will not be enough to win today and what it takes today will not be good enough for tomorrow's arena. Learn from what it took to win today then concentrate on tomorrow's business.

In Los Angeles during the 1984 Olympic Games, two athletes I worked with qualified on the same day in their respective events for the finals which were the next day. Martin Girvan in the hammer and David Ottley in the javelin had both done well to make their finals. After qualifying, Martin was met by back-slapping team-mates who stayed with him almost until he went to bed celebrating a very real achievement – making an Olympic final. David had a quiet dinner, talked through what went right and wrong and cleared his mind for the only competition which mattered now – the final. Martin's pals unwittingly took his eye off the ball. David won the silver medal. Getting into the final means little once you're there. Fighting well in the final means everything.

The two most critical differences which separate you as athletes who are mountain people from those who hide in the valley, I've kept to last.

The first is that winners are people of **vision**. They are dreamers who constantly visualise achievement and success whilst asking themselves 'what if?' They have and use imagination to anticipate and create change. George Bernard Shaw saw it this way:

Some men see things as they really are and ask, 'why?'
I dream of things that never were and ask, 'why not?'

That's not to say that winners do not have a grip on reality. You know the easy part in life for you is to have a dream. It gets harder explaining that dream to others. But you can do it. It is harder still getting others to believe in that dream so much they all want it to become reality. But you can do that too and when you get that far, delivering it is easy. Winners, you see, don't just dream about it and talk about it – they do it.

The second is that winners take **the risk of winning**. The greatest excitement in life is the risk of going for the win. Here you are taking things right to the margin, so the safety cushions are gone. We're not talking here about being careless or hoping for a miracle. I've nothing against miracles, but in my experience the 'miracle option' – relying on blind luck to see you through – is no option at all. You have no choice where miracles are concerned. You can't plan for them and you can't count on them to deliver when you need them. Instead, the risks you take as a winner are calculated. They test your next level of competence, they challenge your capacity to make the right decisions and the right value judgments under new levels of pressure. Your whole life is preparing you for that next step, that next test.

Long after he retired from playing first division football, Jimmy Greaves was reminded that he continued to hold the record for the highest number of goals scored in a season. In typical style, his reply was, 'I also got another record that same season – the highest number of goals missed!' Jimmy understood that the goal won't be scored everytime you take a shot, but it certainly won't be scored if you don't take any. Knowing that he might miss didn't stop him taking the risk of scoring.

In the 1991 Tokyo World Athletics Championships high jumper, Dalton Grant decided to pursue his interpretation of the risk of winning. His best jump all season had been two metres 30 centimetres but in the Tokyo final, he didn't start jumping till the bar reached two metres 31 centimetres. Such a decision carried with it a huge risk. The blow to Dalton if he had failed to make even one jump in Tokyo after all the preparation he had put in would have been devastating. Dalton was well aware of this but as he put it, 'Two metres 30 centimetres will get me nowhere today so why play around with two metres 30 centimetres? I know I'll need to top my best

*One learns people through
the heart,
not through the eyes and intellect.*

Mark Twain
(page 118)

*The way a man wins,
shows much of his character.
The way he loses,
shows all of it.*

Canute Rockne
(page 33)

to be in the real fight for medals so today I'm going for that.' He cleared two metres 31 centimetres and then went on to jump two metres 36 centimetres – an incredible new British record. Although this earned him fourth place it was only two centimetres – less than an inch – below the winning performance and an outstanding personal victory.

Dalton's example is a strong lesson. We can all be winners, we all have it within us to be mountain people, so what are you waiting for? Get out there and take the risk!

CHAPTER THREE

THE TEAM

'Team effort', according to Michael Winner, the film director, 'is a lot of people doing what I say.' I'd like to see him tell that to a Daley Thompson or a Linford Christie.

The first lesson for any team coach is that each member of a team must be treated as an individual and that each individual must be allowed and encouraged to make his or her own statement. The difference lies in the context in which that statement is now made. It becomes part of a broader statement – that of the team. One athlete's statement now helps others express theirs; the statement of the team as a whole helps the individual to express his or hers. Team-work, then, starts with the concept of developing individual athletes to get the best out of themselves, then developing those skills which athletes require to apply that 'best' to the corporate endeavour of the team.

This is not always as straightforward as it sounds. For instance, what is best for the team may not always be what is best for the athlete. One of the greatest skills of the team player and one of the hardest to develop, is actually when *not* to apply your strength in the interest of the team.

In the 1991 Formula One Grand Prix race at Imola, the two McLaren drivers, Ayrton Senna and Gerhard

Berger were well in control of the race in first and second place and in the later stages had begun to stretch their lead. Gerhard then started to chase Ayrton, and as he did so, received through his earphones advice from Ron Dennis that Ayrton's engine was giving trouble. Had Gerhard continued his charge he would probably have won, but in the fight with the leading car, there was also a probability that Ayrton's engine would give out and he would then fail to finish. Of course, that would have been a win for Gerhard and McLaren but it could also mean that instead of having the McLaren team first and second, McLaren would only have first place and lose the manufacturer's team points for second. A tough decision for anyone who is, in every sense of the word, a mountain man. He held off his charge and made sure that his team enjoyed the success it deserved.

This great play was rewarded later in the year at Suzuki, in the second to last race of the season, when the two drivers again found themselves in a one-two situation. By this time Ayrton was well on his way to victory over Nigel Mansell in the driver's world championship. With Mansell beaten, and McLaren cruising to one and two, this time it was Ayrton's turn to move over. Gerhard went on to win the race, Ayrton to take the driver's championship and McLaren to win the constructors' competition.

The first step towards mastering the complexities of team-work is to recognise that there are actually two kinds of team effort delivered, respectively, by cooperative teams and contributory teams.

Cooperative teams

These are the most obvious kinds of team. They feature in sports such as soccer, American football, basketball, tennis doubles, hockey and rowing eights. They are also the types of team you see in many work and business situations, typically within departments or divisions. Each member of these teams relates to, relies on, cooperates with and supports other team members in pursuit of team objectives. Each must perform to capacity, yet needs the others on a moment by moment basis to let them do so. Developing cooperative team performance is not simple. In the words of Casey Stengel, head coach of the New York Yankees, 'The easy part is getting the players. Getting them to play together – that's the hard part.'

Athletes in cooperative teams must first be able to keep their eye on the ball and apply their own skills to best advantage. They also, however, have to learn to think for each other – to know and understand their fellow players. Through this they learn where and when to bring a colleague into the game so that the colleague can be most effective in terms of applying his or her skills and therefore most effective in meeting the team's objective. You don't pass the ball because you're stuck with something to do with it. You pass because you know that the person you're passing to can use the ball better. You learn to read the game so that you know when to lead and when to help another player take the lead, so that you know when to change your position to

49

give the other player a choice of action or to increase your own choice.

The best team players do not jealously protect their personal territory in the game. They do not project an attitude of 'It's not my responsibility', 'It's not my department'. If a colleague is caught out of position the ball is yours. If you are taken out of position your colleague covers. I've often thought about just how old this idea is. Back in the days when my ancestors fought with shields and claymores the shield protected your left side and the right side of the warrior on your left. You trusted the man on you right to do the same for you.

Trust in our team-mates is something every team player must learn. I remember watching a practice game of American football and the quarterback, my son, had been sacked for the fifth time in the afternoon. His dignity was bruised and he decided to have words with his own linemen about the job they were doing. 'Sorry Frank, we're trying.' 'Trying? – sure, it feels like you're trying to get me killed.' On the next play the opposition almost had a free run at him and he was flattened. As he was picking himself up one of his team-mates called over, 'Now, *that* is what it feels like when we're trying get you killed, Frank!' After that he learnt to trust that they were giving their all and to button his lip.

This kind of trust I'm talking about can often be encouraged by appreciating the efforts required of our team-mates. Johan Cruyff developed his youth teams at Ajax and at Barcelona by obliging the players to play in positions which were not their normal positions.

How far you go in life depends on your being tender with the young, compassionate with the aged, sympathetic with the striving, and tolerant both of the weak and the strong. Because sometime in life you will have to be all of these.

George Washington Carver
(page 67)

'How can you talk about 'total football' if your players don't understand the game from every point of view? You have to be able to read each situation not only from your position, but also from that of your colleagues. Each pass of the ball by your team or by the opposition, changes the situation. You cannot adapt quickly to these changes if you constantly think only as a sweeper, or as a striker, or a defender. You must prepare from the start to change with the situation so that you always remain in control.'

Each player, then, spent some of his developing years learning the game from the perspective of his team-mates. I cannot think of a stronger commitment to the concept of a cooperative team than cultivating such a collective understanding.

In business, such an approach has also been success-fully applied. Expamet plc, after retraining managers, placed them in other departments to put newly learned skills into practice, prior to being returned to their own. This initiative, 'Managers in action', built a strong team understanding.

When you get the cooperative team effort right there can be no doubt that the whole is greater than the sum of the parts. The Soviet Union had athletes in neither the 100 metres nor 200 metres finals in the 1988 Seoul Olympics. They did, however, win the 4 x 100 metres relay gold. Equally, the doubles events in Grand Slam tennis tournaments are far more often won by doubles specialists than by superstar combinations. In fact, one of the greatest challenges to any cooperative team is what happens when a superstar does join its ranks. By superstars here, I mean players who are exceptional compared with existing team members. More often than not such new arrivals know their own worth and have the 'rough edges' that go with that knowledge. To complicate matters the new player may well have been brought in to 'save the team', at least in the eyes of the headline writers, putting him under pressure and straining his relationship with his team-mates from the word go. How do we go about fitting the pieces of such a team together? The chief coach of the French rugby club, Béziers, puts it this way, 'When a genius comes to play in my club, he first learns how to play with the team. The team then learns how to play with the genius.'

Each individual team member has to be developed at his or her own level and this is as true for the exceptional player as for his team-mates. The elite player must have his or her elite needs met, but all other players must likewise be developed by building on their strengths for their motivation, for their self-esteem and, of course, for the team. The process needs to be as painstaking as putting together a jigsaw puzzle. Every piece has its own place. You take time to work out which piece goes where otherwise you damage the pieces and the picture is spoiled.

Despite what journalists may like us to believe, no team wins because of one individual. There is a hidden lie in the commentator's excited cry – 'Lewis wins the relay for USA', 'Rush wins the match for Liverpool', 'Montana is named Most Valuable Player'. What could Lewis have done if the three other athletes had not got the baton to him with a chance to beat the other athletes on the anchor leg? What were the other ten Liverpool players doing for ninety minutes? No one player is more valuable than the others who have played their hearts out for their team. Exceptional abilities a team player may have – more valuable than their colleagues they are not. There is no class system in a team. The team wins – not one or two of its members. You'll never get the best from your players if the team does not share this belief.

When the team is being developed as a whole the coach works to create a climate where each player, irrespective of his ability level compared with colleagues, feels that he has equal responsibility for the team's performance. This is a difficult climate to maintain, because it can never be true that all players are equal in terms of their personal combination of technical, tactical and performance abilities. Because this is the case, it is clear that the coach cannot approach the development of all players in the same way. You cannot develop 'unequals' by treating them as 'equals'. On the other hand, each player must have equal opportunity to develop his abilities. So equal opportunity and responsibility do not, in fact, mean treating everyone the same. It's a tough business being a team coach!

It is a truism both in sport and in business that when everyone thinks the same no one is really thinking. You need every member of a team thinking how best to make their abilities count for the team and how to develop those abilities. You need every member of a team thinking how best to help his or her colleague make their abilities count for the team and how to help in their development. It requires a special blend of accepting responsibility for your own actions and performance and for those of your colleagues who make up, with you, the team. When everyone shares this responsibility each is at once a winner and part of a winning team. This applies whether that team is a sports team, a business team or that largest of all teams, a nation. I believe, for instance, that this approach has been at the root of Japanese business achievement in the arena of the international market place for many years.

Contributory teams

In these teams each athlete makes his or her contribution independently of others. It's almost as if each athlete is in a separate competition. There is no cooperation required to produce the team's result. The team's performance is based on the aggregation of all the athletes' individual contributions. It is probably best explained by using the example of the European Cup competition in athletics.

In the men's competition there are twenty events contested by eight national teams. Each team has one athlete in each event. Eight points are awarded for first place, seven for second, down to one point for last place. A disqualification counts zero. The winning team at the end of the two days of competition is the team with the highest total points score in the competition. (In the separate women's competition there were sixteen events but this has now been increased to seventeen. The competition is, otherwise, the same as the men's.) A win in the 4 x 400 metres relay, then, is worth the same number of points as a win in the high jump. Athletes in these events compete at different parts of the stadium and on different days. They make their individual statements in their separate events but the points they score for the team carry equal weight in determining how the team fares in the cup competition.

In business, contributory teams might consist of individual agents, or consultants out in the field covering different geographical areas. The company's 'team score' is achieved by adding together the 'points' achieved by each 'athlete'. Only in this case, the points are the number of sales or contracts or customers. These points determine the company's overall level of achievement or profit in the arena of the market place.

In large companies it is common to find a mixture of cooperative and contributory teams. Within a specific department such as personnel or marketing the effort might be cooperative. Between such departments, however, the team-work is more contributory, with each adding their points to the company total. The situation is further complicated in those cases where athletes who are in sales forces are actually encouraged to compete with each other as part of the motivational climate that business represents. It's often possible in situations like this to end up wondering who's actually in your team and, therefore, on your side. Keeping sight of who your team-mates are and whether your effort is cooperative or contributory becomes crucial at this point if you're to continue to be an effective team player.

There is nothing more difficult to take in hand, more perilous to conduct, or more uncertain in its success, than to take the lead in the introduction of a new order of things. Because the innovator has for enemies all those who have done well under the old conditions and only luke warm defenders in those who may do well under the new.

Machiavelli
(page 12)

NASA, the United States space agency has been a model of team-work in action for many years. It is almost impossible to grasp the degree of team-work required to produce functional reliability of 99.9999+ % in launch machines with six million component parts. The story of a visit by President Kennedy to the Space Centre at Cape Canaveral in the early years of the programme perfectly illustrates the degree to which team-work was felt at NASA. Kennedy had already met with astronauts, scientists and technicians when he came across a man pushing a broom. 'And what's your job here?' asked the President. 'Sir, I'm putting a man on the moon,' was the reply. It's my guess he meant what he said because he was made to feel involved. He was a member of the same team as the astronauts themselves. The 'small step for a man and the giant leap for mankind' were as much his as they were Neil Armstrong's at 02.56 GMT on July 21st 1969 – and the leap was for team-work.

Compare this example with that of those executives and managers who walk past the person in reception with little more than a word. Very few, if they ever encounter cleaning staff, would recognise the person in overalls as working for the same company, the same 'team' as them. Yet the person in reception is the first representative of the company when a customer walks through the door. That person can make the customer relaxed and welcome so that he or she feels that this visit matters to the company and that the company cares. The person in reception is, then, as important as every other athlete in the company team. Exactly the same is true for cleaners, maintenance staff, and just about anyone else you can think of.

The first time I learnt this lesson myself was when starting senior school. My grandfather took me aside on my first day and handed me this piece of advice: 'There are only three people you must be sure are on your side at school. The janitor, the cook and the groundsman, after them the rest are academic.' At the time I thought he was crazy – surely, the people I needed on my side were the teachers and the headmaster – but I soon realised he was right. How many times did the kitchen staff find something for me when I was late for lunch? And where would I have been without the janitor to let me in early in the morning when I wanted to catch up in the library for the time I'd spent the evening before practicing sprints on the groundsman's well-kept track?

In sport, the national team may seem only to comprise athletes, managers, coaches, administrators, doctors and physiotherapists at a championships. But it also comprises the secretarial staff back at the office arranging everything from the quality and quantity of kit to the team's official documentation. Each deserves to feel that he or she matters because you and I show that we are interested in them. The same principle can even be extended to the supporters who follow a team. In 1990, Andy Roxburgh, the manager of Scotland's football team, sat with his players having failed to get the result they wanted against France in Paris. Chins were near the floor. Outside, the Scottish supporters were still singing and cheering. Andy said, 'Listen boys – the supporters are still on your side.

We're still in the event to make the finals. I'm going out there to face them – who's coming with me?' The supporters were ecstatic to see the players who went out with him. The gesture recognised them as part of the team, a part that stood by the players in success and failure and who by their support could make a difference.

How to keep sight of your team and your team-mates? – that was the problem to be addressed at the team talk on the morning of the first day of the 1989 European Cup. For the first time in the history of the competition the team was capable of challenging the two teams who were normally first and second – the Soviet Union and East Germany (as they were then). Athletes in track and field athletics are competing as individuals 99% of the time. They may be called a 'team' but to be honest, in most respects, that simply comes down to having the same flag on your vest. What I was wondering at that meeting was not only how to help the athletes get the best from themselves but also how to ensure that each understood that his performance was as valuable as that of every other person in that room. Only by helping them understand that, I felt, could I be sure of their maximum motivation to achieve not only individually for themselves, but also for the team as a whole.

'Over the next two days you have a fourteen point mountain to climb. It's a mountain, because it will be tough, and you'll have to take the risk of winning. But you are mountain people – you know how this feels and you know what to do. It's fourteen points, because that's the difference between what you are worth on paper and what the Russians and East German's are worth. What this means is that if you, Shane, are worth one point and can turn it into two, it gives us the same extra height up the mountain as if you're worth seven points, Kriss, and can turn it into eight. And as for you, Linford, eight points is what you're worth and today, like any other day for you, second best won't be good enough.'

Shane Peacock turned one point in the hammer to three. Kriss Akabusi turned seven points in the 400 metres hurdles to eight. Linford Christie delivered his eight again. Everyone pulled his weight and went for the extra point. The team were European Cup Champions on the Sunday evening.

This result qualified Great Britain for the World Cup competition in Barcelona several weeks later. This competition is spread over three days, but the basis is the same. In the hotel, after getting back from a rain drenched third day, there were celebrations because although the team had finished second behind the USA they had again beaten East Germany. I wanted to reinforce a point:

'It has come to my notice that we beat East Germany by two and a half points. I want to know who is responsible for those two and a half points!' Every hand in the room went up. The point was, I think, made. In order to get the best from everyone in your team you must let each athlete feel that he or she belongs and they will only feel that if they feel they have value. Every single member of a team matters. Every point, every extra point, matters. Each athlete must know that this is so and must be helped to develop to make it so.

Keeping in mind who our team consists of and how to make our players feel they belong to the team is particularly difficult when a team's line-up changes. For one very good reason or another, teams are, of course, constantly changing their players. The reason may be thrust upon the team. For example, in cases of injury/illness, retirement, transfer or an athlete's loss of form. Or the reason may be an active decision to change composition in the short or long term. This might apply to 'blooding' new athletes for the future, resting established athletes in preparation for a key competition or meeting the specific demands of a particular competition or opposition style of play.

In major athletics championships the rules state that you may only use a total of six athletes in the relays. Four athletes run in a relay team, so this allows you a maximum of two changes. In 4 x 100 metres it is a dangerous business to play around with your 'preferred four', because this 'cooperative' team requires some very tight pieces of coordination and training. The USA 4 x 100 metres team decided to rest Carl Lewis in the 1988 Olympic Games semi-final to keep him fresh for the final. The idea was, on the face of it, reasonable because Carl had had a hard programme – 100 metres, 200 metres and long jump. However, the margin for error under pressure in 4 x 100 metres relay baton changes is very small. Unfortunately, it became so small for the USA team that it was disqualified, so the well rested Carl Lewis did not get a chance to run in the relay at all.

*If I had eight hours to chop
down a tree,
I'd spend six sharpening the axe.*

Abraham Lincoln
(page 99)

*The most important lesson of all is
that we don't compete in the arena
alone, but at every point in our
preparation too.*

(page 148)

Whatever reason you have for changing the team, and whatever changes you make, the team must still be able to deliver and keep you in the championship that you eventually wish to win. You may well wish to use the specific stress of high level competition for development but you cannot do so if the primary objective of the championship or the business is lost. In general, it is much easier to introduce new members into contributory teams than cooperative ones. For this reason I have always found it easier to use the 4 x 400 metres, with its greater contributory aspect, than the highly cooperative 4 x 100 metres, as a development opportunity for youngsters.

Despite the dangers, however, I do not believe any team can stand still. I've often been advised, 'Don't change a winning team.' Yet despite the risks the fact remains that a team wins on a particular day against a particular opposition. Tomorrow is a different day and the opposition will be different (if only because they've learnt from watching you win yesterday). What's more, the chances are that your own team will be different for one reason or another. It makes sense, then, to keep the team more of a dynamic concept than a static one. It's another way of staying competitive in the toughest of all games – change. It requires high quality in your capacity to make value judgements when calling critical shots under pressure, but it comes with the territory when you take the risk of winning – not just this once, but all the time.

One rule I always try to follow in team selections is involving the reserves. It is always good to agree the team with the athletes, including those who won't compete today. The reserves then still feel a part of the team for tomorrow. Your reserves in this sense represent the hidden strength of the team.

I remember Bill Bowerman – coach at the University of Oregon – speaking to his track squad on their first morning of training: 'Not all of you guys will wear the vest next season. But you'll all be responsible for making sure that the athletes who do are the very best. That's because that's what you are – the very best.'

Clarence Callender is an athlete who is a perfect example of this in the Great Britain 4 x 100 metres relay squad. In 1988 he was called on during warm-up to take Linford Christie's place on the last leg for the semi-final. Linford had to be rested – but Clarence had run last leg several times. He helped get the team in the final, but watched the team win the silver medal from the stand. In 1989 he was reserve at Gateshead for the European Cup team which won that competition and again at Barcelona for the World Cup. With only thirty minutes to go, the first leg runner for Great Britain, Tony Jarrett, pulled out with a hamstring strain. Clarence was brought in and told, 'It's your job to get the baton to John Regis even faster than Tony. You are not a reserve any more – you're the lead off in the World Cup.' He ran so hard he almost made me cry and the reserve team in Barcelona ran faster than the first team had in Gateshead.

I believe it to be so important that reserves know they are part of the team, that team managers now follow an agreed team procedure. When a team wins a medal at a major championships, those reserves who have actually run in a qualifying round or semi-final to get the team into the final, also receive the relevant medal. The team, the vest, continues to achieve and to build for future achievement by developing athletes to accept responsibility for that achievement. The team, then, is a blend of experience and of new kids on the block, and that blend must be constantly adjusted and modified to meet the immediate challenge and prepare for the challenges to come.

Teams, be they cooperative or contributory or a mixture of each, don't just happen. It takes time for athletes to grow into a team – to make their statement in it and for it. Working for yourself is much easier for an athlete than working for and with others. The skills required to think for yourself, for your team mates and for the collective pursuit of a team objective do not just automatically follow because a group of people is referred to as a team. They must be constantly coached and serviced to make the whole greater than the sum of the parts; to make the performance of the team more and more effective; to make the achievement of the team more and more outstanding. You do this by establishing each individual athlete's value in the team context, and by cultivating the culture of team-work as something that is not just a topic of conversation but more like a way of life.

CHAPTER FOUR

THE COACH

How far you go in life depends on your being
tender with the young, compassionate with the aged,
sympathetic with the striving, and tolerant both
of the weak and the strong. Because sometime in life
you will have to be all of these.

George Washington Carver

At some point in our lives we are all athletes, attempting to achieve the very best we can do. Our arena may be sporting, academic or professional. It may even be in the home as we try to be winners as husbands and wives and parents. Less obvious, however, is the fact that we are all at some point in our lives coaches to other athletes. These may be new team-mates, younger colleagues, staff in our departments, even our children. To continue the habit of winning throughout our lives we need to win as managers and parents and even as friends and that means winning as coaches.

What does winning mean for a coach? Just as it is the athlete's objective to make a total statement about himself or herself in the arena, it is the coach's objective to guide the athlete towards making that statement. Since I believe that real achievers, the people who win in their arena, are made not born and that their 'making' comes down to quality coaching, achieving the objective of being a great coach is, for me, a statement in itself. Don't underestimate it. It's a uniquely difficult statement to make.

'You can achieve anything in life provided you don't mind who gets the credit,' were the words printed on a card on Ronald Reagan's desk and it's a good motto for all who would be coaches. In my romantic youth, when I was just starting out as a coach, I described the process as beginning with the coach giving light to the athlete, and moving towards the point where the coach became a mirror reflecting the athlete's own light to make it even brighter. Certainly, for the early stages of this process, the coach has control. But the purpose of exercising that control is to pass it to the athlete in the latter stages. This is the hard part. Being asked to coach someone is a terrific honour and compliment, but it is also a major responsibility. Part of that responsibility is to apply your wisdom to know when to pass on control and to have the courage to do so. It is because this is so hard to achieve that different coaching systems and styles have been developed over the years.

Coaching systems

There are three main coaching systems which serve as the vehicle for preparing or developing athletes to make their 'total statement': the escort system, the transfer system and the partnership system.

Winners are first and foremost individuals, because winning singles you out.

(page 28)

When a genius comes to play in my club, he first learns how to play with the team. The team then learns how to play with the genius.

Chief Coach Béziers Rugby Club
(page 53)

The escort system

This is where the coach works with the athlete from the time the athlete takes his or her first steps in the sport to the time they take the steps of the Olympic rostrum. The system has its champions and has produced excellent results for such great athletes as Seb Coe and Steve Cram. It works by providing individual athletes with top quality personal attention over many years, but demands that the coach is always ahead of the game in the athlete's development. Not every coach can achieve this, and for every Peter Coe and Jimmy Hedley, coaches to Seb and Steve, there are many who unwittingly make their athletes victims of their own limitations. Although every generation is likely to throw up one or two spectacular instances of the escort system the almost superhuman mix of experience and expertise required in one person to meet an athlete's requirements throughout a whole career of achievement means that it is likely to become rarer and rarer at the highest levels of sport.

The transfer system

This system avoids the difficulties of the escort approach by introducing more coaches. An athlete will work with one coach at one stage in his development, then be trans-fered on to another who's a specialist at the athlete's next level of development as he progresses. It's a system we've all been through at school where new teachers take you to new levels of development. In sports such as tennis this is quite normal. In track and field athletics, in what was formerly East Germany, the same coach might operate at two levels. For example at the Jena Club, Erich Drechsler worked with beginners in all disciplines before they moved on to one or other of the club's specialist coaches. He was himself one of those specialists in jumps, coaching such world class athletes as Rolf Beilschmidt (high jump) and Heike Drechsler (long jump). The only real problem with this approach is that there can be a break in development when moving from one coach and learning to work with someone new. Recognising the point at which to hand over can be crucial and varies from individual to individual. If transfer comes at the same time as a step up to higher levels of competition it can be doubly difficult and valuable time and commitment can be lost. However, when coaching staff work as a team, the system works well.

The partnership system

Under this approach the athlete works closely with one personal coach, but together they work in partnership with other specialist coaches for certain areas of the athlete's development. Anyone who has ever been a parent will understand the partnership system. The specialist coaches we're most familiar with are called teachers.

This kind of partnership marries the best elements of the escort and transfer systems while avoiding their main drawbacks and for this reason is my own favoured system. In particular, it has allowed me to coach athletes in a wide variety of disciplines and I have used it over the years with Daley Thompson (decathlon), David Ottley (javelin), Dalton Grant (high jump), Kim Hagger (heptathlon),

Yinka Idowu (long jump), Boris Becker (tennis), Jeoff Thompson (karate), Katarina Witt (ice skating) Mark Maclean (squash) and Leslie Beck (ski slalom).

I believe that all three systems, depending on the athlete, coach and situation can be equally effective. However, despite the past successes of escort and transfer systems I think the partnership system will become more and more the norm as achievement at the highest levels demands faster and faster access to specific resources and expertise needed to prepare individual athletes.

In the case of teams, the partnership approach has long been recognised as essential by head coaches. They may still direct operations and apply their specific coaching skills but every head coach, today, knows he needs a sizeable partnership team to meet the needs of every athlete and the team as a whole.

At a major championships such as the World, European or Olympic, the British athletics team has a Head of Delegation, a Men's Team Manager and assistant, a Women's Team Manager and assistant, two or more doctors, four or more physiotherapists, an Administrative Officer and assistant, nine or more coaches and the Director of Coaching. In addition, athletes may request that personal coaches, physiotherapists or religious advisers are at the championships. Coaching the team has itself become a team effort. Everyone on the coaching team has been involved prior to the championships themselves in discussion or implementation of the preparation reports produced for every

*Look abroad through
nature's range,
nature's mighty law is change.*

Robert Burns
(page 7)

*In a changing world,
change is the only thing
you can really count on
and change is on your side.*

(page 7)

major championship. No one is starting from scratch in terms of the specifics of the competition. On arrival a thorough briefing is given to air all relevant information and get everyone up to speed with their own jobs within the team. A chance is also taken to talk through again how we operate as a team, because preparation team members change and you can't assume for a moment that everyone shares a common view of what a team is, let alone how this one works. I particularly like to get together personal coaches and other personal support people to make sure that everyone knows what's happening in terms of all the various procedures and working relationships which apply to this particular championship. To summarise, quality team leadership, if it is to meet fully individual team members' needs, needs a quality leadership team.

Coaching styles

Whichever system of coaching you choose there are four common coaching styles that all good coaches apply during an athlete's development. These are directing, coaching, supporting and counselling. The latter stage is where, in management, you are in a position to delegate.

The athlete's statement in the arena is the athlete's not the coach's. So the coach must prepare the athlete by developing him or her towards a freedom and competence to make that statement. The four styles actually coincide with four stages of athlete development towards that point.

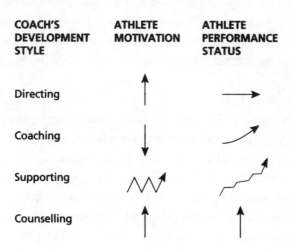

COACH'S DEVELOPMENT STYLE	ATHLETE MOTIVATION	ATHLETE PERFORMANCE STATUS
Directing		
Coaching		
Supporting		
Counselling		

Directing style

When an athlete or new member of your team meets you for the first time, motivation is high. After all, the athlete knows who you are and that you are going to help him or her fulfil their ambitions. On the performance front the athlete may well be better than his peers – this may be what has made him want to develop in this sport or business and come to you in the first place – but chances are he won't be too developed yet.

Against this background the coach sets the ground-rules for how the athlete and coach are to work together. The coach is very much in charge at this point, applying experience and expertise to making early assessment of where the athlete is heading and planning how he or she will get there. Early personal preparation plans leave very little room for interpretation, with the athlete following them almost as a set of instructions or orders.

Coaching style

Although performance status begins to improve, one feature of this next stage is that motivation drops. There are two reasons for this in my experience. The first is that most of the novelty of what was a new situation has disappeared. The next is that I've never met anyone who improved as fast as they thought they should.

The coach needs to change tack to combat this and introduce what I call a 'sleeves rolled up' approach, applying specific technical knowledge and people knowledge to help the athlete work on strengths and accelerate development where this is needed. Importantly, the coach begins to involve the athlete much more in designing his personal preparation plans. These now proceed with some feed-back, more like demonstrations and examples than orders. They are not given life only by the coach. Part of the heart beat is the athlete's.

Supporting style

Now things start to get up to speed. The athlete's performance status really starts to climb. It does so in surges rather than along a steady gradient. The surges coincide with an alternating pattern of work designed to improve performance and work designed to stabilise existing levels of performance. Motivation varies, with far more ups and downs. But the biggest difference now is that control of things rests more with the athlete. He or she has accepted greater responsibility for performance development and for motivation. Now the athlete understands where he or she is heading and wants to be involved in how to get there. Coaching style is adjusted again in this new climate. The athlete is fitted into the role of decision-maker and the coach works to equip him or her for this role and to guide the athlete through the more difficult ones. Coach and athlete design, evaluate and review preparation plans together. This certainly is not the easiest stage. The athlete has to take a few bumps and bruises in exercising responsibility for his or her decisions, and the coach's supportive style must strike a balance between catching the athlete before a fall; picking the athlete up after a fall; and letting the athlete pick himself up. This involves sensitive judgements in using the opportunity of problem situations to develop resilience whilst avoiding serious motivational injury.

Counselling style

Here motivation is high, performance status has taken off, and the athlete is, to all intents and purposes, coaching himself. The strong relationship between coach and athlete built through the first three stages continues to grow, but while the coach may continue to design the preparation plan with the athlete, this is the point at which the coach or manager can begin to delegate responsibility with the athlete making most decisions himself and seeking counsel only as specific occasion suggests. Essentially, by this point the relationship is one we are all familiar with – a friendship between equals.

I had three coaches in track and field athletics. George Sinclair coached me when I was at Royal High School in Edinburgh, Tony Chapman, then Scottish National Coach, coached me after I left school, and Dr Geoff Gowan, now in Canada, coached me through Loughborough College. My days as a track and field athlete are pretty distant memories now, but I still talk through some of my coaching and professional problems with them today. It's as if the coaching style of that fourth stage is the one we'll live with for as long as the friendship is there.

A family friend, Beatriz Bolton, said she wished for me the strength to give my children the two gifts that were mine as a parent to give: roots to grow and wings to fly. I think this captures the process of being a good coach, manager or teacher as much as that of being a good parent. Give strong roots through directing and coaching. Give great wings through supporting and counselling.

I don't think there is any point in discussing which of these styles is more important or effective. All are important when applied at the right level of athlete development, and all are more or less effective depending on the coach's ability to use them. Indeed, the greatest difficulty

What the hell, you might be right,
you might be wrong...
but don't just avoid it.

Katherine Hepburn
(page 184)

I must have a prodigious
quantity of mind;
it takes me as much as a week,
sometimes, to make it up.

Mark Twain
(page 184)

in applying these styles comes in underestimating the intermediate steps and overstressing directing and counselling. There is a real temptation to jump straight from the one to the other, but in my experience this is a serious mistake. It puts athletes at the sharp end too fast and expects too much from them without laying the right foundation. This kind of low quality coaching is unfair to the athlete and unfair to the team they play for. Furthermore, it's expensive in terms of time, energy, emotion and, of course, finance to put things right. The tragedy is that because putting things right more often than not comes back to the same coaches who were at fault in the first place the style used is probably directing again. This can become a very repetitive and unrewarding process.

A coach must learn all four styles, all three systems of coaching, and know when and how to use them. You may be required to apply different styles and systems with the same athlete in different aspects of his or her preparation.

The decathlon with ten events is a classic example of this. In 1986 I was working with Daley Thompson in California. At that time, a directing style was applied to several technical aspects of the 100 metres and 110 metres hurdles, a coaching style to high jump and long jump, a supporting style to most of the track and gym conditioning and a counselling style to javelin, shot and discus. Although the preparation planning had been agreed between ourselves and his training partner Greg Richards, the partnership system was also applied in that

Paul Brooks, pole vault coach at Haringey looked after this event and Art Vanegas, throws coach at UCLA, coached the specifics of his shot and discus.

Different coaches in a partnership system will also apply different coaching styles depending on their responsibilities. Hopefully, however, these styles will be complimentary.

During any championships I like to concentrate on getting the motivational climate right. For this I virtually live in the warm-up area. I hardly ever see the competition itself but I do see everyone before they go into the arena and after they come out. It's the perfect place to encourage, to reinforce, to comfort, and to remind. It is extremely important that every moment is used to keep the motivational climate right. I've often thought that this is very like the management technique referred to as Management by Walking About (MBWA) except it's become CBWA because it's coaching! This 'walking about' approach is very effective in binding people together as a team by helping each athlete understand that he or she matters personally as a member of the team. I'm well aware, however, that Coaching by Walking About can only work well for you and, therefore, for the team, if you are leading a really good coaching team. It's *their* concentration on directing and coaching, and my confidence in their abilities, that allows me to deal with supporting and counselling.

Coaches and athletes

Knowing how to operate as a member of the coaching staff is vital to any modern coach, but of course the most important relationship in a coach's professional life is with his athlete. It is important that there be a mutual understanding in such a situation.

On the morning of my first session of conditioning training with Boris Becker I watched him put away the biggest plate of bacon and eggs I'd ever seen and had to voice my concern. 'Big breakfasts don't give me problems,' was his only answer. We went to the Monte Carlo Country Club in his car and I remember he was playing an Eric Clapton CD. Boris asked me what sort of music I liked and I said I'd just been to a Whitney Houston concert in London. We arrived at the club and got down to work. To be fair to Boris he took everything I threw at him and would not let the session beat him, but on a couple of occasions he looked quite ill. For lunch we went our separate ways and when Boris picked me up again for the afternoon session I wasn't all that certain if we'd be working together for much longer! As the car pulled away he switched on the CD. It was Whitney Houston. Next morning he stuck to cereal and toast. We'd both learned a lot about each other over those twenty-four hours! The basis of any athlete's achievement is a quality relationship with his coach. He'd let me know early that he wanted to have that basis. (I should point out that this is the same athlete who, on realising I was not a good passenger in a fast car, took his Porsche up to 200kph on the hill from the harbour to the palace in Monte Carlo. At one point I thought we were going to go straight off the top and land in Africa!)

A quality coach-athlete relationship needs work from the coach's end too. Creating the right atmosphere for achievement is a large part of coaching and without doubt lets coaches do their job more effectively. It's not difficult to do, but it does have to be worked at all the time. For instance, we all know that people who feel good about themselves perform better. The simplest way to establish a quality relationship with an athlete is by working out what sort of things make that athlete feel good about himself or herself. This doesn't take a degree in psychology. The easiest way to approach it is by thinking about what makes you feel good about yourself.

I'm pretty sure the one thing we all have in common, is that we like to be remembered and noticed. Payton Jordan, when he was head track and field coach at California's Stanford University, used to greet each athlete with a moral boosting, 'Hi Champ!' It might be an obvious way of making people feel good about themselves but it's worked on countless occasions. In the words of William James: 'The deepest principle of human nature is the craving to be appreciated.'

You can apply this technique further by remembering people's names. Making a point of showing that you've recognised them and displaying the warmth and pleasure that people know means they matter to you can make a real difference. Use your eyes, use your smile, use your touch, use their name. Having said that, there's little point in being good with names if you've got nothing to say. I like to do a little extra homework before any occasion when working with a team to check my facts about the people in it. If there's a full team involved in a championship that means up to 120 people, from athletes who are first timers with the team, to household names, plus all the supporting staff. I'd like think I've a reasonable memory, but it's definitely not good enough to carry everything I may need to know about everyone in the team. The solution is to write everything down. So much credibility is blown with a careless slip. In track and field, the athletes have a right to expect you to know who they are, what their event is and what level they are at. You are never forgiven for getting these things wrong.

Some years ago an official who was not normally with the team wanted to get more involved in the excitement of competition. The intention was good but the problem was he didn't really know anyone. The first hiccough was to introduce himself to an athlete, who had every right to consider himself to be well-known, then honestly admit that he didn't know the athlete's name. Around the same time he commented to an athlete how well she had thrown the javelin when in fact she was a discus thrower. The athletes concerned, naturally, told other athletes and the next thing we knew each was outdoing the other for stories of the hapless official's blunders. This unenviable reputation once earned was impossible to shake off and it haunted him till he left the sport.

Always design a thing by considering it in its next larger context – a chair in a room, a room in a house, a house in an environment, an environment in a city plan.

Eliel Saarinen
(page 139)

This kind of response is the athlete's equivalent of that old business saying, 'Customers don't get angry – they get even.' We all have personal experience of these situations. In my own case, I have never forgotten the credit card company who held my account for many years and the accusing letter they sent me on the one occasion that I overspent my limit. I was quite prepared to admit that I was in the wrong. An emergency had arisen while overseas with the team and I had had to pick up a bill personally. But considering that I banked with the same people, that I had never missed a single repayment and that they had been sending me letters inviting me to raise my credit limit for years I thought the tone of their letter was out of order. Still, they got what they wanted. I never exceeded my limit with them again. I turned my card in that very day and have been telling anyone else who was considering taking this card of my experience with that particular company ever since. If you're in any doubt that this makes a difference just ask yourself how you would feel if I had had a similar experience as a customer of your company and named you here.

In the day to day situation, it is, of course, important to have such basic knowledge in your head when you speak to your athletes and staff, but the critical difference in terms of letting people know that you are interested in and care for them individually is having some detail of what and how they are doing. People feel especially good about themselves when you can go beyond the general, almost courtesy, comment or compliment, to be specific and positive about them personally. You're showing that you recognise something that makes them different, and winners, of all people, are that. I've yet to meet an achiever who is not that little bit different. The difference is what I call their 'rough edge'. Maybe this is what people are acknowledging when describing someone as a 'rough diamond'. Wherever that expression comes from, it suggests someone who is precious yet unable to fit into the mould of normality. The biggest mistake you can make as a coach is to try and fit them into the same mould as other people. Of course, it would make life more comfortable if you could do this but no one should come into coaching for a comfortable life, and fitting winners into moulds will usually make them the same as everyone else. Winners are one of a kind, and that means they are 'different' and must be coached and supported to make their statement. The easiest way to do this is to recognise them for the special individuals they are.

I've got an easy job when it comes to focussing on individuals and letting athletes know that I'm aware of who they are and what they've done. In track and field athletics each athlete has what we call a 'life-time best performance' or 'personal record'. Also, in any given season or year, he or she will have a 'season's best performance'. Moreover each athlete's personal coach is, naturally, identified with these performances. So for athletes and coaches, these measurable personal achievements afford a basis for comment which will make them feel good about themselves.

Information like this is always available if only we're observant enough to pick it up. It can come from conversations with athletes and coaches about themselves and about who's doing what elsewhere. Because there's so much change taking place for each of us in the course of one week, let alone a year, the pursuit of what's happening must be continuous. During the heat of a championship you prick up your ears even more to make sure that you know about and can comment upon a result – the positive parts of it and the parts that are going to require work.

In 1989 during the European Cup at Gateshead, Fiona May was upset at her long jump performance. I'd already seen some of the event on the TV in the warm-up area and had heard from a colleague that Fiona had been unnerved in the arena by the East German long jumper. As Fiona prepared to jump, the East German athlete would sprint on the runway parallel to hers and within her field of vision. She needed to be picked up. She also had to channel her frustration: 'You wouldn't want to win with tricks like that, would you?' She didn't, and I knew her own values in life would never let her. 'You shouldn't feel mad at how far you jumped, because you always give it your best shot. You should only feel mad at letting the East German's antics put you off.' She now had something else to sort out with her coach, and could re-focus on the task at hand; getting as far along the long jump pit as possible.

If you're paying attention it's easy in sport to know an athlete's strengths and the strengths of personal coaches and team preparation staff. This is crucial because I believe you should always begin your coaching from a position of strength. What's going right should always be the starting point, not what's going wrong. In this way you confirm or re-establish self-esteem and the confidence and security that comes from believing in yourself as a winner. This really establishes the environment for achievement and builds that extra bit of trust which frees athletes to discuss those aspects that require development and to be more positive in their approach and involved in their development. Going at things the other way round simply confronts athletes with what they can't do well and probably don't like doing because that's so. This focuses on failure and lowers morale.

In the winter of 1987 I was working with heptathlete, Kim Hagger. Because she required technical coaching in shot put, a specialist coach looked after this event. One evening I surprised even myself by turning up at the training venue one hour before I was due to work with Kim on her hurdles and long jump and took the opportunity to sit and watch the shot put session. I'd watched the coach at a distance before and knew that he deserved his excellent reputation. However, that evening I think he may simply have been too aware of a spectator and got nervous. Kim went into the circle and put the shot. 'Right elbow dropped,' he said. She walked out, picked up the shot, went back into the circle and tried again. 'Not fast enough with the right hip.' She tried again. 'Left shoulder is falling away.' And again. 'Left foot's in the bucket.' It went on like this for twenty or thirty minutes. Her chin got closer and closer to the ground until finally she kept looking across at me for a smile, or some bit of reassurance. She couldn't wait to get into some hurdling for a chance to enjoy the confidence of working on something she was better at.

I feel really strongly about keeping things always on the plus side. You can pick up very early in a conversation whether at home, in training, or in the work situation if someone is down. The rules are straightforward at that point – no negative points even if you know something needs to be worked on. Sometimes this will be when you feel you're probably in as much need of encouragement as your athlete but it's worth finding the energy to help the athlete first. This extends as far as changing what you planned to do with the athlete if that's what it takes to ensure that he or she will at least come back for the next training session excited by the prospect of its challenge.

It's not difficult to keep up someone else's enthusiasm provided you remember Clarence Day's line, 'You can't sweep people off their feet if you can't be swept off your own.' Project excitement and energy and you'll find it's infectious.

Despite all the above, whether we like it or not, occasions arise when it's clear you have to sort out a problem that's well and truly on the athlete's side. It's not a mistake or decision that's gone wrong The person concerned is simply out of order. You can't duck the issue, so it's important to know how to deal with it. You're pointing out that he or she has done something wrong and you don't want it repeated and at the same time you don't want to destroy all the good work you've

A good manager can step on someone's toes without messing up the shine.

David Shaw
(page 92)

I've never met anyone who improved as fast as they thought they should.

(page 76)

already done in building your relationship. The approach needed here was best described to me by David Shaw when he was General Secretary of what was then the British Amateur Athletic Board. 'A good manager can step on your toes without messing up the shine,' was how he put it.

When actually dealing with the situation there are a few rules worth noting; speak to the athlete in private; deal with the problem immediately; be specific on the point of issue and go for the ball (the behaviour), not the athlete (the person); use only first hand knowledge; explain the consequences of the behaviour at issue and agree how to avoid it happening again; finally, once dealt with, it's over. The only other thing I would say is that it's important to remember what it is like to be on the receiving end of one of these. If the person concerned is going through a bad time, it's not for a good coach to hit him or her when he or she is down. If or when the problem crops up again deal with it then but don't refer to the one that got away.

There are always going to be athletes whose respect and ambition you can advance, but what about the athlete who is 'elite', who has got to the top, where does coaching fit in here? Many such athletes think they no longer need coaching and as a coach it is often tempting to agree. Trying to coach elite performers is hard work, especially if they don't want your help or think they know better. Often, too, the returns are less obvious with an athlete at the height of his powers than with a newcomer who still has everything to learn. Against this is the fact that you don't come into coaching for a comfortable ride. Nor do you come in to sit in the best seat. Ego's have to accept standing room only. Remember those rough edges! As a coach your name is more likely to hit the headlines when the team loses than when it wins; for getting it wrong with an athlete once, than when getting it right a hundred times.

The rough edges of each elite achiever with whom you work will leave you with a few cuts and bruises but you need to develop your ability to handle this. You'll grow in the process and become even better equipped to know when to be strong in coaching or strong in supporting. Those edges are what make such athletes special in the first place but they must not be allowed to harm the athlete himself or herself, nor must they harm the corporate spirit that makes a team. Here's where your judgment is tested most as a coach. Always be sure, whatever your decision with that rough diamond, that your course of action does not have your own comfort as the motivation behind it.

I am not convinced that people leave one company to work for another or switch the team they play for or do anything else that suggests loyalty has gone out of the window, purely for reasons of economic or other reward. The latter are normally factors which may finally tip the balance in deciding where to go after deciding to leave. The real reasons are, for example, because what they have at the moment fails to provide the challenges they need, or because they feel they do not have the support to achieve their ambitions, or because they do not share the values of the company, or because they don't feel cared for as individuals. We're not talking here about those people who will move and continue to move for reasons that are to do with economic advantage. Nor are we talking about people who have to move for reasons that are nothing to do with the quality of opportunity, coaching, care and so on of a great company or team. For example, if a partner has to relocate in his or her job or a change of lifestyle is sought then these moves are just part of life. We are talking about people who joined our team or our company because they wanted to work with us and for us, who chose us over some other company, team or coach.

Each challenge, once met, ceases to be a source of motivation, so the key to keeping all of our athletes, from the beginners to the elite, rests in identifying new challenges, coaching them to meet these challenges and providing whatever support it takes to help them achieve new goals.

Finally, in any relationship between a coach and athlete there must be honesty. On the coach's part this must include the honesty to admit that you're human. A willingness to review your own methods and approach from time to time does not put a question mark against you for competence. It puts an exclamation mark against you for innovative achievement. Coach and athlete know that decisions made are right far more often than not. By admitting that it's a learning process for you, too, you actually share with your athlete the risk of winning that comes in taking up the challenge of change. It's the best way I know of establishing mutual confidence. You are pointing out that decisions can be wrong sometimes, but the moment you know that this is the case, you admit it, correct it, make a new decision, and head on up the mountain. The idea is not to get the same thing wrong too often! You are also pointing out that while you both are in the business of doing things right you are also in the business of going the extra mile to get things right when there's a problem. You learn to take personally the effectiveness of your coaching as measured by the quality of the athlete's statement in the arena. You learn not to take personally the cuts and bruises. In the end you must coach with the same courage the athlete puts into competing.

Most coaches arrive at the decision to work on this or that aspect of an athlete's preparation by interpreting the same sequence of events: evaluate the athlete, the situation and relevant resources; agree an objective; agree tasks to meet the objective; agree exercises and activities to achieve the tasks; build all of these into a plan with a timetable; deliver; re-evaluate and go through the sequence again.

The best coaches are those who have gone out of their way to maintain high learning momentum in the technical business and in the people business. The learning is initially mostly reading, listening and watching. This is what I think of as the early analysis phase, where you don't want to get too far away from the basic programmes and practices which other coaches have used with regular success. It is also the phase where coaches may slow their own rate of development by being afraid to make a mistake. The next phase is where coaches shift from analysis to action. They continue on the book learning side because that should always be the case, but now the emphasis is in learning through experience, through taking risks. These risks are calculated, of course, not careless. This is where you begin to personalise your coaching.

Anatolyi Bonderchuk, former Olympic hammer champion, and certainly one of the greatest coaches I have ever met taught me most about having the courage to take these risks. In 1979 he flew from Moscow to Edinburgh in the coldest January I can remember to address the European Track and Field Coaches Association about his methods. Part of the address was to be a practical session outdoors at Meadowbank Stadium. When we arrived there the snow in the stadium was almost knee deep. Finding the circle was not going to be too hard because it had to be inside the safety net. Finding the hammers after they'd been thrown was the problem that would occupy us most!

As one of the stadium grounds staff started to clear snow out of the circle, Bonderchuk asked for the brush and insisted that he cleared it personally. Once done, he stood in the circle to test the surface by going through the foot movements of the event. He wanted to know for himself if the surface was slippery or slow before he

*We are or we become those
things which we repeatedly do.
Therefore excellence can become
not just an event but a habit.*

Albert Einstein
(page 35)

*Excellence is an art won by
training and habituation.
We are what we repeatedly do.
Excellence, then, is not an act
but a habit.*

Aristotle
(page 35)

watched the young hammer throwers who had come to demonstrate.

When the session started, Bonderchuk moved about thirty metres away from the circle whilst most of us were much closer. It was only later when working on a few details of each athlete's technique that he joined us.

'You have to get a feeling for the athlete's technique as a whole. If there is a problem, a little one or a big one, you'll spot it straight away because either the big picture looks right and has rhythm and balance, or it seems slightly out of focus, or it just isn't right at all. It's not possible to do this by standing too close. You have to stand back to get the big picture. Here you can begin to think, "If I do this, what will I do to that picture?" You get a better feeling for the consequences of each coaching decision at a distance. When you have decided what to do, only then do you get close enough to work on what is to be done. As you work, you gradually pull back again to see what's happened to the picture.'

At that time, I could only think I'd read the wrong books. He'd run through the same sequence we all do, but in his own personal short-hand. It was this preparedness to put so much of himself into his coaching and his bravery in trusting his own instincts that made him an elite coach.

CHAPTER FIVE

THE PERSONAL PREPARATION PLAN

If I had eight hours to chop down a tree, I'd spend six sharpening the axe.

Abraham Lincoln

You cannot hope for high quality achievement with low quality preparation. This is true whether we are talking about the achievement of an athlete or a team. It is true whether we are planning for the short term, say the tactics for a particular match or for the long term, such as the training schedule to improve technical performance. In either case good preparation frees energy, abilities and concentration for the work of the arena. They are not wasted dealing with those problems which could be anticipated and eliminated beforehand.

How often have we all found ourselves at a loss for words in a meeting, stuck over a problem in an exam or out of breath on the sports field only to kick ourselves for not preparing better. Even if we come second today, knowing that we have prepared ourselves honestly means that, instead of looking back, we can start looking forward, start planning for next time. In this way we continue to move towards our goals but the detail of how we do so changes by the year, by the season, or even, if necessary, by the day. This is the first rule of planning – that it remains flexible.

It's a bad plan that admits no modifications.
Pubilius Syrus

This flexibility is needed when we encounter set-backs, but even more so when we achieve our goals. For instance, I used to think of the early planning for an athlete as planning for a journey. I would identify our destination then decide on the route. Training would be the vehicle and the date of the next championships would be our estimated time of arrival. I would allow time for wrong turns and expect to re-plan the route for diversions. This seemed to me to be a very neat way to describe the process but it fails in one very important respect. The problem is that the journey towards achievement is not like any other journey. As soon as you arrive at one destination it transforms itself from a terminus to simply another stage on a road to greater achievement. Achievement is a journey without an ending and the hardest part of planning for this journey is how to arrive at one destination and not only look forward to the next, but be equipped to handle that next stage.

The first time I became really exposed to the need for this was in the 1981-82 season and I must admit I didn't get things right. I was coaching a young Scottish sprinter, Cameron Sharp, and the goals for 1982 were to make the Athens European Athletics Championships in both the 100 metres and the 200 metres, and to run 10.35 seconds for the 100 metres and 20.70 seconds for the 200 meters in that year. Cameron's previous best performances were

10.38 and 20.92 respectively. The year plan commencing October 1981 was prepared and the early winter work was started. In January 1982, he ran indoors over 60 metres. This competition was used annually in his programme to assess progress over the first three or four months of training. Previously, his best was 6.90 seconds. In 1982 he produced 6.69. Clearly our destination had to be changed. Cameron's potential performance come the summer could be quicker than we had planned for and some thought had to be given to providing a higher quality of competition so that he could realise this new-found potential. The changes were made and the results kept on improving. I was naturally delighted for Cameron and pretty pleased with the work of his coach!

Even in Athens all was going well until a moment just after the semi-final of the 100 metres. He had finished a very easy second on 10.38 having run 10.28 in the previous round. We were heading for the locker room where he would get a massage and prepare for the final in ninety minutes time. We'd walked about twenty metres when he suddenly said, 'You're not saying much, coach.' He was right. I really didn't know what to say. Cameron now had a destination that he'd never headed for before as an athlete, and I'd never headed for before as a coach. I would have known what to say if he'd been struggling because we'd been *there* before! But at that moment everything had gone right and for the first time in my life I was coach to someone who had a clear shot at a gold medal in a major championships. Of course, I'd prepared the athlete to get to this point but I'd failed to realise that I had to prepare for the next step too.

Knowing what to do when you're winning and have exceeded your expectations is in many ways harder than when things go wrong and you're losing or when they go according to plan and you make expected progress. To finish that story, I didn't get it right first time. Cameron finished fourth in the 100 metres final. Two days later, however, he ran a lifetime best of 20.47 to get the silver medal in the 200 metres and two weeks later ran 10.20 for a lifetime best in the 100 metres at Zurich. I suppose it was at least reassuring that you never stop learning and I was still able to do so!

Adaptation energy

This comes down to the energy which the athlete has available to adapt to the demands of the plan. I think it best to consider the energy situation as a balance sheet.

The **energy income** is from the foods we eat. For most of us it is sensible to keep carbohydrate intake high (about eight grams per kilogram of body weight per day) and the fat/oil intake low (less than twenty percent of our daily calorie intake). This means it's okay to hit pasta, boiled potatoes, rice, rolls and preserves, but better to play down the fry-ups, cream, cheeses and dressings. If you want to keep weight stable the energy income must not exceed the energy expenditure. Whilst on the subject of diet, I should also mention protein, vitamins, minerals and fluids. Because your energy expenditure causes a bit of wear and tear on your body machine, you

*Wanting to win is an appetite
that can't be satisfied.
It means wanting to keep on
winning forever, whatever it takes.*

(page 26)

*Winning is not a one time thing
it's an all the time thing.
You don't win once in a while;
you don't do things right once
in a while. You do things right
all the time. Winning is a habit.
Unfortunately, so is losing.*

Vince Lombardi
(page 35)

need good quality protein (one gram per kilogram of body weight per day) for growth and repair; a regular daily intake of vitamins and minerals in the form of a multi-vitamin and mineral tablet, or drink (and extra vitamin B and C in periods of extra energy expenditure); and a litre of fluid per day (you will, of course, need much more fluid if you spend a lot of time in offices or on planes with dehydrating air-conditioning, in warm weather or if you are suffering with cold or fever). This said, adequate energy income normally is assured by a balanced and thoughtfully designed diet.

The **energy expenditure** is the cost of how we live our lives. I like to think of it as having two general components – lifestyle energy requirements and adaptation energy reserves.

Lifestyle energy requirements

We all need a certain amount of energy to accomplish the normal tasks of life and this amount will vary from individual to individual depending on their lifestyle. Pushing a barrow clearly takes more physical energy than pushing a pen, but energy is not only required for muscular work. A student athlete's performance in training and in competition is always poorer during periods of intense study or during exams. We've all experienced that drained feeling after weeks of intense work pressure. Mental and physical work both draw on the same energy pool. Our normal personal lifestyle, then, has an energy cost, but this is not the only energy demand we may meet.

Top: Frank and Daley Thompson – 'Who's the greatest athlete you've ever seen? You're looking at him, buddy.'

Right: Frank at one of his motivational presentations – 'I believe we should adopt a coaching style of management for preparing people to win the game of change.'

Top: Frank discusses training with Boris Becker while Seb Coe looks on.

Bottom: Frank puts Boris through his paces – 'He took everything I threw at him.'

Top: Frank and Gerhard Berger – 'In every sense of the word, a mountain man.'

Right: Frank in festive mood with Jeoff Thompson, karate champion.

Top: Frank and family – Linda, Cara and Erin – enjoying life in the middle lane.

Bottom: Frank, Boris and Daley – 'The basis of any athlete's achievement is a quality relationship with his coach.'

Adaptation energy reserves

Change brings the need to adapt to new circumstances and that requires energy, too. The greater the degree of change, the greater the energy cost of adaptation. Athletes need access to high adaptation energy reserves to cope with the demands of new and harder levels of training. We all need access to high adaptation energy reserves to cope with the demands of change at work and at home or in the event of crises.

Because there is clearly a limit to the amount of energy we each possess, the adaptation energy reserve will be high if the lifestyle energy requirement is low. Conversely, there will be little energy left to meet adaptation needs if lifestyle energy requirements are high. What we each need is a situation in which we can meet both lifestyle and adaptation requirements without running into an energy overdraft. When this happens we can shift from being in control to being in distress – not the way to climb mountains!

I believe that this need not happen and that having a well constructed personal preparation plan will make sure that it does not happen. My reasons for this realistic optimism are these:

1. **Personal management.** Each of us, in managing our lifestyle more efficiently, will use less energy and, therefore, have more adaptation energy reserve available.

2. **Personal fitness.** Personal fitness programs designed to equip us to meet the demands of our lifestyle, again reduce energy requirements in this direction, leaving greater reserves.

3. **Personal training.** Because training programs can adapt us to new challenges, to higher work levels and to change in general, what we've adapted to becomes part of our lifestyle. So what once required energy to be drawn from our adaptation reserve is now accommodated within our lifestyle requirement.

The key, then, in our game of change is always to have a high adaptation energy reserve to win in it. The question is, how do we adapt?

Imagine you were asked to jog for thirty minutes. If this were not part of your normal routine, extra energy would be expended dealing with muscular activity, increased heart rate, increased breathing rate and so on. The **immediate effect** would be energy expenditure and movement towards fatigue as your adaptation energy reserve was reduced. When you stopped jogging, the **residual effect** would be for heart rate, breathing and so on to continue operating to try and get life back to a normal state. In other words the movement is towards recovery. Adaptation energy reserve is also being tapped here. It's a similar process to what happens when you arrive home from a day of crises at work and your brain is still turning over office problems. You not only act to deal with the physical or mental challenge as it happens but also after it's over, your body and mind keep up the effort to deal with it. This is what we call 'super-compensation'. Your body and mind have raised their game. It means that the next time you're faced with the same challenge you will be better prepared. It will not represent the same threat to your normal state. If this super-compensation is repeated over a period of time, that particular change ceases to be a threat at all. It becomes part of normal routine and any energy needed is dealt with as part of lifestyle energy requirement. Think of how taxing it once was to learn to drive a car or operate a word processor or find your way around in a new town. Then reflect on how each of these has simply become part of normal life. Adaptation energy is no longer required to deal with it and becomes available to deal with new challenges. For a coach this is the time to revise the preparation plan.

This is quite a straightforward idea as long as we're dealing with one change at a time. For example, if the objective is to develop strength in the legs, an exercise programme can be prepared with progressions as the coach continues to take advantage of one super-compensation stage after another. This is the **cumulative effect** of training when you are pursuing continued increase of leg strength. The same principle applies, of course, if the objective is increased endurance, mobility, speed etc. and is pursued through a specific training programme. I guess this principle was what Milo of Croton had in mind back in the days of the ancient Greek Olympics. He wanted to be strong enough to lift a bull, so he found a calf and lifted the same calf each day as it grew and grew to eventually become a bull.

Life gets more complicated when a number of changes require adaptation at the same time. In athletics training programmes it is frequently the case that general strength, specific strength, endurance and technical competence are all being developed within the same programme. For example, Daley Thompson's weekly programme was quite a busy one.

Complications arise when development of, say, endurance, actually interferes with development of a specific strength; and where the cumulative effect of pursuing development on all these fronts may run the athlete so low on adaptation energy reserve that he or she becomes distressed and breaks down.

You develop someone by coaching him or her to adapt to the changes which you build into his or her development plan. This brings me back to my reasons for 'realistic optimism' which I'd like to expand here. A good plan has enough **balance** to present change, even across a range of disciplines, as a series of challenges. Balancing your plan so as not to exhaust all adaptation energy reserves at once is crucial and this must be done with sensitivity to the needs of each individual. The right balance for Daley is not necessarily the right one for Boris. This balance can be even harder to strike if the athlete is facing changes across the whole spectrum of his life, not just in his sporting or business environment but also at home. Here adaptation energy can be drained in ways beyond the control of some coaches. It is for this reason that I believe the coach must take account of all aspects of the athlete's life when designing the preparation plan.

TRAINING PHASE PLAN   Name (Athlete/~~Team~~):

Phase No: 3

DALEY THOMPSON

Commencing: 24-03-1991

Ending: 25-05-1991

No. of Weeks: 9 WKS

Objectives:

1) SPECIFIC STRENGTH
2) GENERAL STRENGTH
3) SPECIFIC RUNNING ENDURANCE
4) COMPETITION SPECIFIC PREPARATION.

Programme/ Microcycle		Cycle of 7 Days Repeated 9 Times				
Day	Unit 1	Unit 2	Unit 3	Unit 4	Unit 5	Unit 6
1.	TRACK ①		HIGH ①	DISCUS ①		STRENGTH A①
2	HURDLES ①		POLE ①	JAVELIN ①		STRENGTH B
3.	TRACK ②		LONG ①	SHOT ①		STRENGTH A②
4.	HURDLES ②		HIGH ②	DISCUS ②		STRENGTH B
5.	R E G E N E R A T I O N.					
6.	T 6	SPRINT comp		LONG comp	SHOT comp		END SPRINT comp
7.	S T	HURDLES comp		POLE comp	JAVELIN comp		END RUN comp
8.	TRACK ①		POLE ①	SHOT ①		STRENGTH A①
9.	HURDLES ①		HIGH ①	DISCUS ①		STRENGTH B
10.	TRACK ②		LONG ①	JAVELIN ①		STRENGTH A②
11.	HURDLES ②		POLE ②	SHOT ②		STRENGTH B
12.	R E G E N E R A T I O N					
13.	T 6	SPRINT comp.		LONG comp.	DISCUS comp		END. SPRINT comp
14.	S T	HURDLES comp		HIGH comp.	JAVELIN comp.		END. RUN comp.

The safest way to offset these unknown factors and maintain a balanced plan is to build into the preparation a healthy allowance of **regeneration** activities. I like this word better than 'recreation' or 'recovery' because it feels more active and constructive. Regeneration activities do not restrict themselves to variations on the theme of physical exercise. They include everything that allows you to build or rebuild yourself – the aesthetic as well as the athletic. Spending time with loved ones, reading, listening to music, walking, sailing, painting, gardening – anything that lets you get back to yourself for a while is valuable and helps build your adaptation energy reserve. I believe that an effective regeneration programme built into your personal preparation plans is critical to maintaining balance and is central to the concept of 'time management'. There's a limited amount that you can do as a coach or even as a friend if your athlete is undergoing personal problems, but the one thing you can do is give him time to work on them. Manage time to make room for regeneration and you'll head off the crises that might unexpectedly drain your athlete's adaptation reserves.

The real keystone of boosting these reserves is by improving the athlete's **fitness**. Clearly the fitter an athlete is the more easily he will respond to change and the less adaptation energy he will use. In fact, a programme of exercise designed to meet the needs of your life is one of the few things that will actually improve the capacity of your adaptation energy tank. To do this effectively, however, it is important to consider what we mean by fitness.

*Not all of you guys will wear
the vest next season.
But you'll all be responsible for
making sure that the athletes
who do are the very best.
That's because that's what
you are – the very best.*

Bill Bowerman
(page 65)

*You can achieve anything in life
provided you don't mind who
gets the credit.*

(page 68)

Traditionally, fitness is, of course, related to physical performance and health. As such it is normally considered to be the product of regular exercise. I used to think that 'being fit' was a pretty straightforward concept. I knew what I meant when I said that Daley looked fit, that my Dad looked fit, that one player in a team was fitter than another and so on. But then it occurred to me that 'being fit' was different from person to person. Daley looking fit has a different meaning from my Dad looking fit. The concept is not quite so straightforward.

Caledonian Television runs a series of programmes called 'Sport in Question'. The idea is that the audience put questions to a panel who respond with personal views. On one occasion I had the privilege of being on the panel with Terry Butcher (football), Gavin Hastings (rugby) and Hugh MacIlveny (journalist). An old chestnut of a question was posed by the audience: 'Does the panel not think that if rugby players and football players were as fit as track and field athletes they would be more successful?' Gavin Hastings' response was, 'I'm not sure if Linford Christie would remain fit enough to run 9.92 seconds for 100 metres after a couple of hard tackles by David Sole' (Scotland's then rugby captain). The point about fitness is that it means just what the word says it means; being fit, being suited for something. Fitness then can never be an absolute quality. It is always defined by what it is you need to be fit for. A sumo wrestler is obviously not fit for distance running, nor is a tennis player fit for world class snooker. It is pointless to compare one athlete's fitness against another's if the achievements they aim for are different. This is why it is not realistic to approach your own development, or the development of your athletes and teams as if preparation plans can be bought off the shelf to be applied to people who are, likewise, off the shelf. There are no shelf people.

Personal preparation plans must be designed to extend the concept of fitness in practice to something which develops each athlete individually. All aspects of that person should be considered and developed through the plan, because each aspect influences the others. It is, then, comprehensive but unique to each athlete, and the coach takes time to ensure that this is the case. Per-Olaf Asrand (Sweden), one of the finest minds in the world on exercise physiology put it this way: 'Exercise will not put years on your life, but it will put life in your years.' Whether fitness for you is related to objectives in sport or business, vocational or personal well-being your own exercise programme should be built into your personal preparation plan to enhance your adaptation energy reserve.

Designing a plan

When designing any personal preparation plan there are three main stages to be considered.

1. Decide what point the athlete is starting from. This is the equivalent of your **starting blocks**.

2. Decide what point the athlete should be heading for. This is your **finishing line**.
3. Draw up detailed plans for getting from start to finish. This is **the race** you plan to run.

This check list combines an evaluation procedure and the setting out of a plan of action. The trouble with evaluation procedures is that most people tend to view them in a negative light. When you were in school, did you see the teacher's job in marking your exam paper as that of passing you or failing you? – of finding out how many thing you got right or finding out how many thing you got wrong? When you meet with your line manager for a performance review, do you approach the situation with the words of that old prayer running through your mind: 'Forgive me for those things I've done that I ought not to have done and for those things I've not done, but ought to have done?' Perhaps it would be better if performance reviews in business were called 'development reviews'. As a coach, or a teacher or a manager the purpose of evaluation should be to make you more effective in developing people. The outcome should always be a plan designed to help the athlete prepare to meet his or her objectives. Built into this is the idea that the coach and athlete are on the same side. They share the same common goal of preparing the athlete to achieve. Nor is this evaluation procedure a one-off. Periodic development reviews are fundamental to high quality planning to meet new goals. This is the spirit in which to approach the first part of preparation plan design.

The starting blocks

Every coach or manager I've ever worked with has an individual approach to assessing strengths and qualities to be developed. Most of them are extremely effective and I've come to the conclusion that the best approach is your own, or the one you're comfortable with, provided that you continue to look for ways to develop it further. When starting work with national athletes I try to evaluate them under three headings: lifestyle management, performance management, and medical management. Currently these three headings are each addressed in a British Athletics Federation programme funded by the Sports Council, called 'Managing Achievement'.

Lifestyle management

Lifestyle management embraces financial planning, career planning and family and personal management.

By **financial planning**, I mean the business of controlling your outlay and keeping it roughly in line with your income. It is generally recognised that money matters are responsible for some of the greatest stresses in modern life and this is true for the highest achievers even in those fields where the highest achievements come with the highest rewards. For international athletes, where the sums of money can be very large and the period over which they are earned relatively brief, these matters can assume great significance and can distract them from their performance in the arena. It is often assumed by spectators that athletes are somehow above the everyday problems we all face, but they have mortgages like the rest of us and families to support. As a coach it is worth establishing at the start of any preparation plan if your athlete feels secure about his financial position. If he does fine, if not you may need to think about ways of helping him manage these matters more confidently. For my athletes, I recommend a visit to a financial advisor. For an employee, a company might offer similar services but is also in a position to directly solve financial problems either at a service or at an incentive level by offering advances on salary, additional leave with pay, interest free loans, or even a pay rise. Looking both at financial planning and higher salaries as rewards to bring forth the best from an employee are just some of the ways in which managers can be more creative as coaches.

Career planning is closely tied to financial planning. It is important both for amateur athletes who support themselves through full-time jobs – needed for the money but often hard to reconcile with training and competition schedules – and professional athletes who may need to plan for a second career after their athletic one has ended. It's been an interesting and challenging part of my own work as a coach to help develop athletes still at college with their first jobs on their mind as well as those studying for higher professional exams and those who are at once both world class athletes and very successful business people. Others have had conflicts with their employers or been worried about their businesses if self-employed. In general, it is as well to show

Customers don't get angry –
they get even.

(page 86)

Customers support a brand
in exactly the same way
that fans support a sports team.

(page 191)

some interest in this aspect of an athlete's life even if it is going well. If it is, it will probably strengthen him if he's finding competition tough in his sport; if it's not, you need to avoid the loss of confidence in one area spilling over into your arena.

People's money and their jobs are often very personal areas. They are often discussed only with immediate family who are also, of course, intimately involved in such management. **Family management** certainly includes making time for demanding relationships with partners and children, but also the more mundane tasks of taking an active part in family responsibilities; everything from paying the bills on time to painting the house. I know that for some people, the family side of things is considered quite private, as if what happens here has no bearing on the rest of their lives. It is not my intention when helping people design preparation plans to intrude on this private territory but the fact is problems in these areas can't always be left outside the arena of achievement. To the extent that this is true I try to take a sensitive interest in the lives of athletes. Coaching is a scientific discipline, but that doesn't mean that I don't agree with Mark Twain's words, 'One learns people through the heart, not through the eyes and intellect.'

One example of a lifestyle crisis I encountered involved problems with money, career and family management. An Olympic medalist confided in me that due to an injury which had taken him out of competition for two years, his savings were down to zero, and his monthly committed expenditure was more than double his sponsorship income. He did not want to take a job, because it would interfere with training and physio-therapy visits. His wife was expecting their next baby in a few months. He figured if he could just get back on the track he could earn enough to get out of the red. An injury had interfered with the pursuit of athletic achieve-ment as a result loss of income from his running caused family pressures and damaged personal self-esteem. This in turn put pressure back on his running to make it simply a source of income and not pursuit of further Olympic success, which would bring reward both in terms of personal achievement and, indirectly, greater financial return. I figured that earlier advice on the diffi-culties he had would, at least, have let me get expert counselling for him on money management and how to turn things around. Pride and embarrassment made sure that the situation reached the crisis level before he sought any advice. Ultimately, whatever help I could have given in this area relied upon the athlete being trusting enough to open up his personal world to me as a chief coach. Believe me, this was not nearly as easy for him as it would have been had I been his personal coach.

Coaches and athletes often become close friends as they work together, but it is also important that at the very start they share certain **personal values**. These values and principles to which we are committed colour our approach to how we live our lives. The fact is, however, that we are probably only aware of what they are when we come across a person or organisation whose values are in conflict with our own. For example, in my business, I still feel it almost as a personal insult when the opposition play as if rules are there to be tested or as if one object of the competition is to test the powers of observation of the referee, judges or umpires and their capacity to interpret the rules. When establishing the base on which the preparation plan is to be built, you need to have some idea of where the athlete's coming from in terms of values and principles otherwise you really cannot communicate at the same level. In my opinion, you'll only get real commitment to individual, team or corporate development when values and principles are more than understood – they are shared. You should then, have some general agreement on matters like trust, integrity and fairness; on concepts such as responsibility and accountability; on the pursuit of individual goals, and working in a team; on complex practical concerns like the balances the athlete seeks between occupation, family and self, or between pursuit of personal advancement and contribution to the quality of life in the community; and on challenge, competition and achievement. Personal care should seek to maintain these values in the face of challenges and keep the athlete in sight of his goals.

Performance management

Performance management begins with a broad overview of the athlete's general fitness level. As we have already established, how fit you are depends very much on what you are preparing for, but in general overall fitness can be broken down into characteristics such as endurance, strength, mobility and technique. Fitness for any one event requires a specific mix of these qualities, but all are important to some extent. As a coach with an athlete on the starting blocks it is easier to judge fitness if we look at these four aspects seperately.

Endurance or stamina, requirements are not the same in the sustained effort over two hours in the marathon as in the intense muscle aching effort of around 45 seconds in the 400 metres; nor are they the same in a year round competitive sport as in a seasonal sport; nor in a tournament as in a one-off event. All athletes, however, need a sound endurance base to be able to get through tough training and practice sessions. Nor is basic endurance just for athletes; we all need the capacity to keep going. Training to develop endurance is the sort of training which improves the capacity of our adaptation energy tanks. We all, then, need endurance training in our personal fitness programmes.

Strength requirements also vary from sport to sport both in nature and degree. Explosive strength is a priority in sports which require players to sprint, jump, throw or strike. Delayed release strength is needed for endurance events like the marathon. Again, however, we all need a sound general strength base in order to learn the techniques required to take part in sport or indeed to do any physical activity. Out of sport, many of us also need that base to compensate for muscle weakness that can arise because of our occupation. Some people can develop rounded shoulders, sagging chest and abdominal muscles because most of their lives are spent sitting behind a desk or steering wheel. So we all need a strength component in our personal fitness programmes.

Mobility and speed are required to play any sport. A football player or tennis player has far less influence in a game if he or she cannot stretch to reach a ball. Moreover, lack of mobility can expose you to greater risk of injury through muscle pulls and so on. Again we all need to have a basic level of mobility developed through stretching exercises, on the one hand to compensate for all the posture habits we fall into and on the other to let us lead a more active life. The need for speed once more depends on the sport. Good reactions and high speed of response in decision making is not only the difference between success and failure in sports such as motor racing and downhill skiing. They can be the difference between life and death. In general terms, speed has higher priority for those who compete seriously in sport than for those who participate in sport for fun. Consequently, for most people speed development has lower priority than endurance, strength, and mobility.

Technique or skill requirements are specific to the sport concerned and the training associated with it. In some sports such as ball games and decathlon, many techniques must be learned and developed. In other sports several techniques are applied in varying combinations to interpret music, such as ice skating and gymnastic floor exercises. One technique may become progressively sophisticated in certain sports such as high jump and javelin. Because exercise is much more fun if it

There's a thin line between believing you can win and believing you can't lose.

(page 39)

No victory is worth having if the opposition isn't worth beating.

(page 39)

can be absorbed within a leisure activity or sport I believe we should each take time to learn those techniques and skills to a level which lets us participate in an activity or sport, and which lets us enjoy the exercise we get in doing so. Techniques must be learned well. This means you need access to good teaching and you need to have a sound general base of endurance, strength and mobility to avoid compensations and compromises creeping in. Poorly learned techniques limit the value you get from them and limit long term development. They also generate injury risk.

Technique is probably the most important performance area to be assessed on the starting blocks. We all need endurance, strength and mobility to increase our technical ability, but it is this ability that is central to our performance in whatever arena. Technical competence is, afterall, what most people get hired for. It refers to the level of your understanding and application of the skills of your trade, your craft, your profession. For some people technical competence requires considerable physical involvement as in sport; for others it requires the most sophisticated mental skills as in scientific research. It may also require a mastery of technology or the ability to concentrate over long periods in such professions as accountancy or teaching.

For a coach, performance management must have two goals: achieving an improved performance and maintaining the potential to improve that performance further. Fitness not only improves your technical ability it also improves your ability to improve. Put another way, energy needs are linked to technical competence and, of course, to those fitness characteristics required in sport. The fitter you are and the more technically able you are, the more work you can do. Not only this but the work you do will be of a higher quality and require less energy. This energy is then freed for more adaptation.

The energy demands of our work should always be assessed as part of the performance assessment on the starting blocks. Such assessment should, however, go beyond considerations of adaptation energy and include the physical and mental requirements you face both in moments of crisis and in day-to-day duties. It should include the endurance energy for you to actively and persistently pursue objectives and see tasks through to completion. It also includes the energy demand on you to continually enthuse and motivate others. Every leader I ever met, whether in sport or business regularly pumps new energy into the motivational climate to keep everyone going – including themselves.

A final area for performance management is in the relationship between individual athletes and a team. In such cases, it's clear that any personal preparation plan must be designed in association with that of other team members where preparation relates to the team. This does not simply refer to the need for team members to work together and the logistics of getting people together. It must also cover the development of those skills required to work or play in a team. These skills can never be assumed to develop simply through the experience of being in a team. They must be developed and regularly reviewed and serviced. The biggest single problem in developing 4 x 100 metres relay teams comes down to this. The commitment to personal achievement of great sprinters such as Carl Lewis (USA) and Linford Christie (GBR) in their individual events, 100 metres, 200 metres and in Lewis' case, long jump, has represented 99.9% of their development life in track and field. It should not be surprising, then, that neither athlete has found it either comfortable or convenient to always accommodate the demands of being part of a cooperative team. This should be the first thing to observe as a coach starting out with these athletes. It will, then, be as much an exercise of patience and persistence as of team building leadership, to make the parts become a whole.

Medical management

Medical management involves regular medical check-ups, expert scientific support and diet monitoring. We each take our car to be serviced every 10,000 kilometres or so to sort out any small problems before they become big ones. We take our teeth to the dentist every six months for the same reason. Yet, normally we only take our body to the doctor when it's already in trouble. **Annual medicals** are there to prevent trouble. For athletes undergoing very strenuous work more regular medical monitoring on a half-yearly or quarterly basis may be required and a full medical is always to be recommended when setting out on a new preparation plan. In many instances, we need highly specialised opinions on injuries or training programmes and it is vital to have the necessary expertise available at these points. Finally, balance of diet must be monitored as it is crucial for maintaining the energy levels for serious training.

It's part of the coach's job at this stage to make general assessment of the athlete's management requirements and plan to create access routes to the kind of *resources* the athlete may need to achieve his best. Dr Hans Muller-Wohlfahrt, the Bayer-Munich FC doctor once told me that if a Bayern player was seriously hurt in the first half of a game, and the specialist in treatment of that injury was in California, the player could be on a plane out of Munich airport before the full-time whistle went. I like this approach. Our most precious resource – whether in sport or business – is our people. They deserve the best support services. It rests with the coaches in sport and business to identify who can provide those services and create a means of accessing them. This applies to medical, lifestyle or performance management. Such an approach need not require high budgets.

In 1991 an endurance athlete met me to say he would like to go to Mexico City for three weeks. 'So would I,' I replied. 'But it's for altitude training,' he persisted. Of course, I understood that, but I also understood that the air-fare at the notice given was expensive. There was an eight hour time change and an appropriate quality of accommodation and food would not be cheap. On top of this arrangements for local support services would have to be started from scratch. The overall bill was going to be close to £2,000 – money which we didn't have. What he *needed* was access to altitude training. What he *wanted* was to train in Mexico City. I believe that people stay hungrier and sharper if you can give them what they *need* not necessarily what they *want*. A Bulgarian colleague, Peter Bonov, had recently invited me to a training camp at Belmekan in Bulgaria. It had been custom built for altitude running for athletes, offered top medical and sports science support services and food of the quality and quantity which athletes require. Although the accommodation was hardly five star it was pretty good, moreover, it was only a two hour time change. A phone call, a fax, a couple of favours and the deal came out at £750. This was what the athlete needed. This is what he got. Incidentally, I believe that having to fight and apply ingenuity to meet preparation needs such as this, where means may be limited, underlines the importance of skillful planning and this always comes down to the competence and motivation of the people who do the planning.

All these aspects of management should be discussed and agreed with the athlete and it is important that athlete and coach agree on the overall evaluation at the start. They won't be able to share a common goal if they do not share this common beginning. But once this basis has been established it is possible to ensure that the finishing line set by the coach will be one the athlete wants to reach and feels able to reach. With this attitude you're ready to look up the track for the finishing line.

How can you talk about 'total football' if your players don't understand the game from every point of view? You have to be able to read each situation not only from your position but from that of your colleagues. Each pass of the ball by your team or by the opposition, changes the situation. You cannot adapt quickly to these changes if you constantly thing only as a sweeper, or as a striker, or a defender. You must prepare from the start to change with the situation so that you always remain in control.

Johan Cruyff
(page 52)

The finishing line

The first and most crucial stage in setting goals for an athlete is that the goals should be realistic – only one person can win the Olympic gold afterall. This is what the evaluation on the starting blocks is there for. Even then the finishing line is likely to look distant to most athletes and, once it is decided upon, one of the coach's main tasks is to demonstrate to the athlete how to get there. What's crucial for an athlete at this stage is learning to *pace* himself, learning that the goal is not going to be achieved in a day or a week or a month but that work done in these short periods will all contribute to the eventual result. For a coach, however, it is important to understand that most people do not have infinite patience. We all expect a return sooner or later and if this is not forthcoming we lose heart. This is also part of setting realistic goals on a coach's part.

I believe that each of us has only a few opportunities in our life to enjoy moments of really high personal achievement. For some they can occur anywhere from childhood to the late autumn of our careers. For others the arena in which they are achieved can change from one occupation or interest to another. But for athletes there are normally relatively few years – typically between four and twelve – and these are for most sports located in the period from our teens through to our thirties. It's possible within this period to identify the years when an athlete should achieve peak performance. An athlete's 'biggest' years do not come automatically just because he has been in the business for several years. They are planned for by a good coach bearing in mind the timescale from now until these years are reached.

For a track and field athlete peak performance years might come six to ten years into their careers. These are the years in which life-time achievements are attained and Olympic, World and European medals aimed for. These are long term objectives. Before them, however, the athlete may make his first appearences in major inter-national competitions after two to four years of national level competition. At this point it will be an achievement to reach these levels at all and the athlete may not expect to win yet, but the experience gained in the medium term will be vital for achievement in the long term. Even earlier in their careers, of course, the athlete will have competed annually in local competitions progressing up the ladder to national meetings. These will provide him with his first short term objectives.

If we have a limited time in which to achieve, I also believe that we each have a limited 'motivational life' in pursuit of a given field of objectives. In sport, few athletes maintain a motivational life beyond ten years, and these years, of course, need to coincide with the peak performance years and the build-up to them. In business, a similar effect can be seen although the moti-vational lifespan may vary depending upon the profes-sion. It is for this reason that many companies encourage senior and middle management to shift their 'territory' at more frequent intervals than was formerly considered wise. This is seen at the very highest levels in so-called

Cabinet reshuffles. New challenges bring new motivational life and in doing so continue to bring the best from people. Exceeding the motivational life span of people you are attempting to develop, can only damage them and their business. There is no personal drive to take on those challenges that dip into adaptation energy reserve, and the comfortable lifestyle energy requirement begins to be all they want to commit to.

In team sports players may be asked to adapt to new roles to prolong their motivational life. A midfield player in football may drop back into defence; an attacker may find a new career as a midfielder. It's also true that sportsmen in many fields will find management or, as in my own case, coaching, provides the new challenges they need. In business, your peak years can go on and on provided personal preparation plans continue to be reviewed for new challenges and provided the concept of generating new motivational lives is actively pursued. Your personal preparation plan will have its own long term objectives and short term targets and a good work environment should seek to offer you a progression from one to the other.

One word of warning here. Even in the most effervescent period of motivational life, there's a limit to your ability to repeatedly produce quality performance in meeting challenges thrown at you thick and fast. The good coach plans the competition programme to allow sufficient regeneration and new levels of preparation between taxing challenges so that each can be met by the athlete at his or her best. In this way quality can be consistently produced over several years. Failure to consider this can only result in early 'burn out' – the product of persistently operating on a low or empty adaptation energy tank. In teams, you can continue to produce consistently high team performance by resting players and giving development opportunities through competition experience for the next generation. In individual sports, the situation is more difficult but the coach must, nevertheless, design a balanced programme of tough challenge, of low key competition and of regeneration. I suspect this approach would benefit people in business and therefore the business itself, if interpreted to meet their needs.

When pacing athletes I set myself the same question over and over: What is the highest level of achievement the athlete can reasonably expect in the sport? It's a simple question but so is the one that goes, 'how long is a piece of string?' In both cases the way to answer the question is to put it in context. Which piece of string are you talking about? What kind of timescale are we expecting this achievement in? For myself, when I lay out a preparation plan I try to look at achievements that can be made in the next four years, the next year and the next six-eight weeks. The level of achievement in these periods might be result orientated in terms of World/European ranking or placings gained in major championships, or performance orientated in terms of fastest times run or longest distances thrown.

The rolling four year plan

I think the reason I started working four years ahead was because the first year I decided to take this approach was the start of an Olympic cycle and I could see a very clear goal four years hence. Fewer years would, I think make things feel claustrophobic and more years I've not found necessary to date.

Once you've prepared four blank year plans, information is written in as soon as it's available and you soon appreciate the discipline of planning your future life with plenty of elbow room. This discipline brings with it the opportunity to plan for 'next stages' in life (this may extend anywhere from four to eight years ahead). Athletes should be planning for life after sport long before the day arrives to hang up boots, spikes or whatever. There really is no good reason for athletes to be hit between the eyes with the hero-to-zero situation which so often accompanies retirement. This applies equally to students leaving academia for the business world, or to senior members of staff preparing for departure from the company, or to anyone working through their personal performance plan in the sure knowledge that each objective leads to 'new territory' in the shape of promotion, new responsibilities, transfer or whatever. We owe it to athletes, and indeed, to ourselves, to establish this four year discipline of planning to achieve new objectives in even more exciting times ahead.

*Nothing in the world can
take the place of persistence.
Talent will not, nothing is more
common than unsuccessful men
with talent. Genius will not,
unrewarded genius is almost a
proverb. Education will not,
the world is full of educated
derelicts. Persistence and
determination alone are
omnipotent.*

Calvin Coolidge
(page 29)

The year plan

A sporting year varies from sport to sport; from those which have a long period of preparation before a short intense competition season, to those where competitions are spread through seasons lasting two-thirds of the year. Business may require year round competition although the nature of the business challenge may be partly seasonal. Whatever the situation, the personal preparation plan must have periods of steady, lower intensity demand where personal development can be progressed; periods of intense high quality demand where personal performance is put to the test; and periods for regeneration. There are many ways to structure this, but to do so you must first establish where these various periods will occur in the year. You should start with locating in the year plan the high quality demand, then build in the lower intensity demand, then establish regeneration periods. Whatever the year looks like, a preparation plan can and should be designed to meet the athlete's needs. The year is very different for a Formula One Grand Prix driver; a world class ice skater; a world class squash player and a world class karate player. Yet each can pursue a personal preparation plan which meets their sporting objectives, their business objectives and their family/social objectives.

The next six-eight weeks

This is the stage where, in sport, the coach works out what will be done in each unit of training, on each day for the next six to eight weeks. This means taking it down to the exercises, the number of times they will be repeated, how fast, how heavy, how long. The details also include the rest periods between repetitions, sets of repetitions, exercises and units, and so on (the units are then arranged to form a programme in cycles of five, seven or ten days, according to what fits normal routine and gets the best out of each unit). These units and their detail are specific to the relevant objective. They are precisely quantified and are measurable and are built into a timescale. How you arrange what's to be done over the next six to eight weeks is what prepares the athlete to meet the agreed objective of each challenge as it is brought into focus in the course of the year. The collective 'package' of the preparation plan must bring the athlete through to a new level of development building on the previous six to eight weeks and preparing the athlete for the next.

In each of these periods once you have asked what goals the athlete should be set, you need to make the goals clear to the athlete – where, when and what. At the end of any period whatever the result – whether the goals have been achieved or not – the coach and athlete must evaluate what went right and what could have been better. If you're not clear what these goals were at the outset, even if you fail to meet them, you and the athlete will not be able to learn from your mistakes. In each case there will be things that went right to celebrate and plans to be made to deal with what went wrong. Again clear planning lets you recognise what's succeeded and what's failed pretty quickly and this is vital if you have to focus on a new challenge.

In cases of failure, always remember that every opportunity should be taken to make positive reference to the athlete's existing strengths and intention to develop these further. These should be seen as the main building blocks for development. Having done so, the less developed areas can be brought forward in a way that neither depresses nor intimidates the athlete and new finishing lines planned for. In times of success, it is equally important to keep achievements in perspective. This is particularly needed when starting on a new preparation plan when one finishing line must be converted into just another starting point in a new and more competitive race. This can be just as depressing for an athlete as failure if not handled carefully.

As a final point, it is also helpful to develop the trick of keeping the athlete's eye, and your own on the finishing line, you've agreed. That's not always easy. In Split at the European Athletics Championships in 1990 the British team broke the national record for 4 x 100 metres and ran inside 38.00 seconds for the first time. Only one other nation, USA, had done so before that evening. Unfortunately, France ran even faster, setting a new world record. None of the boys felt the elation they deserved to feel in their outstanding achievement. They were only aware of the fact that they did not win and would have felt quite different if they'd run slower and still won. Yet, their achievement was exactly what we had planned for. They had crossed their finishing line. Their disappointment was that someone else crossed the line before them!

The race

*Always design a thing by considering it in its next
larger context – a chair in a room, a room in a house,
a house in an environment, an environment in a
city plan.*

Eliel Saarinen

So far we've looked at assessing athletes, to decide where
they are now and how far they can go in the short,
medium and long term. We're pretty close now to where
the rubber meets the road, designing an actual plan for
getting from starting blocks to finishing line. Every plan
for every athlete will vary depending on the individual it
is designed for, but there are a few general points to any
plan that apply for us all. They should be kept in mind
whether the plan is for the next six to eight weeks or the
next six to eight years.

**You can't work on peak quantity and on peak
quality in the same training unit.** Mostly, you work at
an optimal level of quantity and quality for the athlete to
achieve the preparation or development objective of the
unit. If endurance is the objective the quantity of repetitions is high and the quality relatively low. If speed or
maximum strength is the objective, the quality is very high
and the quantity low. In any phase, it is sensible to keep a
balance between units of work, so that there is an ebb and
flow of quality bias work and quantity bias work. It is
possible by having units with different objectives and
demands follow each other to create a programme where

regeneration is built into the day. I guess this is an updated version of 'a change is as good as a rest'.

Units should be distributed throughout the preparation in such a way that a specific development objective can be repeatedly pursued without the interference which pursuit of other specific objectives may bring. For example, you won't get much value out of a strength or speed unit if it follows on from an endurance unit. Likewise you won't be much good to the family if you're carrying your office on your back when you go out to dinner with them. Yet the preparation objectives may include endurance, strength and speed. These objectives can be met provided units are arranged so that they don't interfere with each other.

Variety of tasks or exercises in units, even when they are in pursuit of the same objective, is good for motivation. Just as there are many ways of developing, say, leg strength there are many ways of pursuing family, personal and job objectives. You should be relentless in pursuit of ideas for variety. On the other hand, athletes like the discipline of routine. Good planning provides variety within a flexible framework of routine.

The demand on adaptation energy from unit to unit can range from being very high to very low. Each athlete has a threshold for being able to cope with concentrated periods of very high adaptation demand. For some this will be two or three days, for others maybe a week. To request even more output once they've reached that threshold is not impossible. We can all squeeze out that little bit more, but to do so repeat-

When people change they should do so to take control – then they're in the winning business.

(page 14)

See the points on the scoreboard as fixed. There's nothing you can do about them. Whether they're yours or the opposition's they're gone – they're history. But there are a lot of points left in the game. They are the future and they're there to be won.

(page 11)

edly will cause the athlete distress. You can't assume that highly motivated people will take the breaks when they need them so you must ensure, for everyone's sake, that regeneration does take place. Athletes should arrive fresh for the challenge of each unit and certainly neither fatigued nor jaded from the previous one. Careful plan design will ensure that this is so without losing the momentum of work each day. Assessment of adaptation energy demand is agreed between athlete and coach. Units are distributed through a day, week and so on in such a way that the athlete is not exposed to a relentless barage of very high demand units to the point where they cannot be completed and there is breakdown in the overall preparation process. In general, try to take an alternating hard/not so hard approach. I like to progress pursuit of different objectives at different rates within a preparation plan to avoid the situation where the cumulative adaptation demand is too taxing. Regeneration is as important to the preparation plan as the hard work.

There is a very good case for going back to fundamentals to gain overview and sharpen up on those parts of our development we take for granted. Jack Nicklaus used to go back to California each year to 're-align his swing' and all athletes should be encouraged to regularly revise their skills. Even if they find that the basics are all in order this is not wasted time. It is always good for morale to remind ourselves of things that we're good at.

Because what we're doing is all about preparing for the challenge of change in a competitive world, the

athlete should have some form of competition or testing. Exposure to the occasional 'shock' of change and contact with high quality performance is needed in every plan. It is important, however, to choose this competition carefully so that it gives a useful test of the athlete's progress, allowing him neither to win too easily nor giving him no chance at all.

The plan: training and competing

With these guidelines in mind you are ready to start on the plan itself. For myself, I always find my plans break down into the same four stages: training to train, training to compete, competing to train, and competing to win.

Training to train

The finishing line you set for your athlete should be challenging. It shouldn't be out of sight, but it should be in the distance. Because of this, to begin with, the athlete may not have the strength or mobility or endurance to learn the skills he'll need to cross that finishing line. Before you can teach him those skills you need a program of general development to prepare him for more specific training later on.

When Ion Tiriac asked me to help Boris Becker, one of the things I was to look at was speed of foot movement. After a couple of workouts it was clear that the problem was not a technical one or a speed one. He could move his feet fast, but not consistently. The problem was more to do with having the conditioning that would allow him to perform the exercises that would help him to develop greater consistency and even faster movement. The initial work, then, was general and involved practices for small adjustments of balance on the move. The idea was to develop the muscles which support the movement we were looking for. You call these muscles the 'synergists'. Their supporting role enables the muscles which are actually responsible for the action or movement to do their job. With Boris, the focus was on small muscles in the foot, lower leg muscles and lower back muscles. Once we got them developed we could start on the actual speed training.

Training to compete

Training can be very demanding, but it is never as stressful as competition. It's part of the coach's job to develop the athlete so that he or she can compete without any kind of technical breakdown in these situations. The stress of competition is what makes it the ultimate test, it is also what brings out the best in people. It is important for a coach to take account of the fact that competition stress will demand more adaptation energy from an athlete than training. It is also important to prepare athletes for changes in the arena. Often these will be down to the conditions or the opponents, but sometimes that unknown factor can be the athlete himself. In competition athletes may find themselves running faster, throwing further and jumping higher than ever before. This is what you hope for, but even this kind of positive change needs adapting to.

Hunches are creativity trying to tell us something.

Frank Capra
(page 194)

Life by the yard is apt to be hard; life by the inch is a bit of a cinch.

(page 18)

In 1986 Daley Thompson was having pain in long jump training prior to the Stuttgart European Championships. This meant that apart from the Edinburgh Commonwealth Games decathlon long jump four weeks before Stuttgart, there had been very little long jump competition or practice. My concern was that he was getting faster over 100 metres and with long jump the next event after 100 metres in decathlon, it looked like he would go into the long jump with greater speed than he'd ever enjoyed before. Of course, more speed is a big asset in long jump but it's a problem if your body tries to coordinate technique at a new level of speed. He ran 10.26 seconds for 100 metres and his previous best in a decathlon was 10.41 seconds. To compound the problem, there was a strong wind assisting the athletes in the long jump. As I watched the event, I could hear echoing round my head, 'The trouble with you, Frankie, is you worry too much.' 'Relax, Frankie, it'll be all right on the night.' 'I'll be okay.' These echoes made me worry even more as it became clear that there were problems out there. Daley had the speed all right, but he was fighting to control his technique. The good news was that everyone else was having problems, so the hardest competitor would win through. He did. Now I still hear echoes of 'I told you, didn't I?'

There's a different kind of feeling that goes through you in competition as opposed to training. The adrenaline is there, and you're balanced on the edge. Daley had learnt how to handle that stress and to cope with the unknown in the arena, even when one unknown element was his own improved speed. There are few athletes like this. As a coach you must take account of the difference between training and competing and prepare the athlete accordingly.

Competing to train

The reason why I'm so sure that achievement doesn't always mean coming first is that every athlete who's ever lived has come in second or third or fourth. Some have even been tail-enders. The point is that competition can also be training. You can learn about yourself, your successes and your failures, but you can also learn from the other competitors. The lesson of their strengths is that you can achieve more. The lesson of their weaknesses is that you can compete with them and win.

Keith Connor won gold for Great Britain in the 1982 Athens European Championships. At the airport on the way home, he reflected on the years which had led up to what had been a really great achievement. 'I couldn't really compete with those guys till I was ready. In each competition I was changing from being a spectator to being a student to being in there competing. It was like an apprenticeship. This time the Russians were athletes I respected but I didn't see them as anything more than people I wanted to beat. Now I was in the competition, actually competing. Then I was just learning what I had to do here.' Keith is one of the few top athletes who have become coaches. He's going to be one of the top coaches, too.

Competing to win

Now you're ready. This is what the athlete 'joined' for and this is what you got into coaching for. I don't need to tell you what it takes to compete in the arena. We all already know that it takes everything we've got if we really want to win – not just to beat others, but to be the very best we can be for ourselves. The most important lesson of all is that we don't compete in the arena alone, but at every point in our preparation too.

Trouble-shooting

These design guidelines have to be pretty general. A good coach will always look for ways to improve his plan as it moves forward. Plans are there to be changed as you learn more about your athlete. They're also there to be changed because we're all human, even coaches! We all make our share of mistakes and we need to see them and alter the plan to fix them. Below are a number of common problems you might meet and how to solve them. I'm a real expert on the solutions – I've made all of the mistakes more times than I care to remember.

Cause The agreed objective was wrong. The objective may be a competition or development work, training or a preparation target etc. The agreed objective was misunderstood.

Solution Discuss with the athlete, agree a new objective and ensure that there is a common understanding of what this is.

Cause The agreed objective was right and understood, but the tasks were wrong to achieve the objective.

Solution Review personal approach to task setting as this relates to the objective, and discuss these and alternatives with colleagues and with the athlete before setting out new tasks.

Cause The athlete's technique(s) is/are unstable under pressure.

Solution Review personal teaching methods as they relate to the technique and discuss these and alternatives with colleagues and with the athlete before applying directing and coaching styles to retraining the athlete in the technique(s). Increase frequency of coach/athlete contact at least in the short term. Train to compete.

Cause The athlete lacks fitness qualities to meet the demands of the task.

Solution Review personal training methods as they apply to each task and discuss these and alternatives with colleagues and with the athlete before deciding new diets of exercise or programmes of activities. Increase frequency of coach/athlete contact at least in the short term. Train to train.

Cause   The preparation plan in general is not meeting the athlete's needs.

Solution   Review personal plan design methods and discuss these and alternatives with colleagues and with the athlete before deciding on design revision. Adjust the plan at more frequent intervals at least in the short term.

Cause   You and/or the athlete have not been able to access relevant support as needed.

Solution   In consultation with colleagues and the athlete identify, recruit and coordinate the support services needed and secure a reliable means of access. Without doubt, access to this support system will be needed by other coaching colleagues and athletes so this solution must be shared with others.

By learning to evaluate and to set goals you can prepare an appropriate personal preparation plan for your family, for your colleagues and for yourself. By mastering the changing relationship between training and competition you can guide them to the finishing line. But the final lesson is to remember that preparing the plan once is not enough. Circumstances in sport and in life in general change. We are agreed that change is the game we must win. Hence it is not enough to draw up one plan once and for all. We need to be drawing up plans, changing old ones, fine tuning and radically reshaping all the time. This happens not only at the end

*The easy part is getting the players.
Getting them to play together –
that's the hard part.*

Casey Stengel
(page 49)

of one plan when we have achieved or failed to achieve the finishing line we set ourselves, but also in the middle of a plan when circumstances change. Preparation planning is tough because it is a dynamic activity, but once we begin it we can revolutionise our lives. Preparation planning links the technical business with the people business. It's that part of coaching which sets the basis for bridging intention and fulfilment. It is not all that coaching is about but it is the body that you will breathe life into with your skills as a developer of people. When you bind these things together – then, you are a coach.

CHAPTER SIX

TAKING THE LEAD

I've always liked the idea of scoring points for both technical merit and artistic impression. It is a clear acknowledgement that there is a difference between mastering essential skills and applying them with flair. Within the framework of a personal preparation plan, quality coaching develops both aspects. You certainly need both to take the lead in the game of change, and take the lead you must, if you are to take the risk of winning. Those who take the lead – who set the pace – are not only leaders in the game of change, but of people in the game.

You already know the essential skills in your chosen arena. You have developed them on the slopes of your own personal mountains of challenge. This chapter looks at how you can apply these skills to the fullest – not just to win but to win in style.

My first yardstick of a stylish winner is someone who not only tops the mountain in their chosen field, but does so while enjoying a life beyond this field. Many are the champions who succeed only by sacrificing friends or family, but in the end it is only the winners who maintain a healthy life beyond their sport that have the strength to keep on winning over the years.

People who take the lead enjoy a unique personal interpretation of time management which permits pursuit of achievement in all three lanes of life's motorway. You see, I think of time management like a three lane motorway. We each have our destination and travel our motorway in the direction of that destination. The outside lane – the fast lane – the overtaking lane – is our occupation or main business. The middle lane is your family, your partner, your friends. The inside lane – the slow lane – is you, that same person I talked about in connection with regeneration.

Now, I know people who live almost their whole lives in the fast lane. In fact, the only time they dip into the middle lane is because someone faster is coming through. They remain in the middle lane only as long as it is necessary to let the person through, then they're right back in the fast lane, head down and really mad at having had to spend time out of the fast lane. Those same people have almost forgotten that the slow lane exists at all. They only remember it's there when they have to put more fuel in their adaptation energy tank.

I guess you're really pleased that you don't know people like that! If you did, I bet you'd remind them that all three lanes comprise their personal motorways; that all three lanes go all the way to their destination; that all three lanes must be maintained in good shape or you meet with contra-flows, diversions or even dead ends.

These people that I know, but you don't, are all probably very good at working out programmes of objectives, tasks and so on for the fast lane. But it seldom occurs to them to approach life the same way for the middle and slow lanes.

I was talking about this some years ago to a group of business people and, as it happened, it was an all male audience. We came onto the following conversation:

'When was the last time you went out on a date with your wife?' I asked.

'You're crazy, Frank. You don't go out on dates with your wife.'

'Why not?'

'Because you do that sort of thing before you get married.'

'Why should it stop there?'

'Because – *you know* – you do things like that, go out together to the movies, to parties, to restaurants, and stuff like that. Besides when you get married you're together at home and you don't have to go out.'

So I explained that I did actually make dates separately with my wife, Linda, and with my two young daughters, Erin and Cara. Of course we also go out together sometimes, but I like the idea of one on one so that I can continue to work on my personal relationship with all three of my ladies. These relationships are precious. I hate to think of waking up some day to find my kids grown up and gone without having every opportunity that's there to be part of that growing up. I want to understand them and hope that there are things about me and my wife they will want to understand. I also hate to think that being married is a different relationship between two people than the one which led them to want to be married. You get married because you've got something going and so when you get married you should want to keep that something going. So I put asterisks in my diary to remind me to 'make a date' and to phone or write to my folks and my sister and those who constitute my 'middle lane'.

'But that's not right, Frank, there's no spontenaiety – it's too contrived.'

'That's true – but it means that I don't just think about it, I don't just talk about it, I do it. *That's* what matters.'

Of course that 'middle lane' is more than a matter of 'dates'. Vacations, visits, purchases, changes in domestic lifestyle, home management objectives and tasks – they're all part of that lane.

People who fail to see the need to consider the middle lane as important usually get the message when a baby arrives to take charge of their life, or when they move house and new domestic routines must be developed.

When you approach this aspect of time management with the same commitment as you do the fast lane, the value to those in that lane, of giving them a higher quality and quantity of your time is returned in more than full measure. They are part of *your* team. When their motivational climate is right, your support for them generates an even stronger support for you. On the other hand, a poor motivational climate breeds discontent which in turn breeds disorder.

Trying to keep your show on the road when there is disorder in this lane is like having a steady leak in your adaptation energy tank. If it continues, over a period of time, progress down your motorway – in any lane –

*Every time you touch the ball
is the most important touch
you'll have in the game.*

Bill Shankley

(page 38)

*Winners remember what the
game is, not what it means,
all the time.*

(page 38)

becomes pretty difficult. Being able to do running repairs is an important skill to have and from time to time it's necessary to apply it well. But if it becomes the rule to apply it rather than the exception, you are in trouble.

These same people that I know but you, fortunately, don't, get it into their heads that if you really enjoy the fast lane, you don't need to think about the slow lane at all. After all, surely you are taking care of yourself when you're having a good time – would that this were true!

One reason you enjoy the fast lane is because you're in control, your motivation feeds off each new success and challenge, you're really ready for every new mile that you have to travel. But it follows as surely as autumn follows summer that a mile will come when you'll feel, 'So what, this is just another mile.' One of those people I know even admitted once that he couldn't remember a stretch of several miles in a journey. He'd switched to 'automatic pilot' so that he could put his brain in another space. There was no excitement, no commitment, no quality in what he was supposed to be doing in the fast lane. I've often reflected that he is lucky to be around to make that admission!

If you don't make time to take time in the slow lane the sparkle that's the real you begins to dim. You only have to ask yourself the same question Bobby Robson posed when manager of Ipswich Town FC: 'Who motivates the motivator on Monday morning?'

The answer is, of course, you. So it should be clear that quality time has to be given to you to keep yourself in shape to do it. You must build into your time management plan a personal regeneration programme for you and your family.

You must, then, focus on all three lanes. Each must have its objectives and tasks based on evaluation of your personal development needs. In sport, it is fundamental to take this approach. No athlete can make his or her statement in the arena either as an individual or a team member, if he or she is trying to resolve difficulties in any of the 'lanes'. The same, of course, goes for coaches! When planning is right, it means that each 'lane' gets your best quality in terms of commitment and energy and, therefore, of concentration.

The best piece of advice I have been given to summarise this was from a friend, Alan Finlay, a manager with BP. Irene, his wife, and Alan had invited us to spend a weekend at their home near Bath. We arrived Friday evening, enjoyed a great supper then sat around the big open stone fireplace exchanging as many reminiscences as there were showers of sparks rushing up the chimney from the logs in the fire. It took till Sunday lunchtime for me to clear my head of all the other problems I had put on the back-burner and Alan had watched this for the best part of two days. 'Frank, you've got to be able to walk away from it.' He is right. By getting your time management right you can do just that. You can compartmentalise your objectives and tasks to such an extent that you deal with each in its own time, giving it a 100% shot. Then you are able to 'walk away from it' and to walk towards a 100% shot in the next part of your life. Quality planning is what makes you able to do so.

To summarise, effective time management is fundamental to your personal preparation plan. That refers not only to your fast lane but to your entire motorway. Remember, when you drive motorways, a problem in any lane will slow down your journey.

Getting this kind of time management right produced a piece of history in the financial services industry early in 1992. In that year, Abbey National's top three financial planning consultants in the UK were women – the very first time in the history of the industry that women had pushed the men out of the medals. When each addressed the audience it became clear that they all shared one common factor in their success – time management. They had each established business life, family life and leisure as the three lanes of their motorway and managed themselves as efficiently as they managed any of their staff. They had made the decision that they were not going to sacrifice their personal lives for their careers and still made it to the top. In many ways they thought that their busy lives outside of the office as wives and mothers, far from being a disadvantage, actually made them more efficient. They couldn't afford to let meetings drag on beyond their appointed time, if they had to collect children from school, or relieve baby-sitters. So they made sure that the business that needed to be discussed was settled in the time allowed and that meetings finished on the dot. They all scored maximum points for technical merit, but they also came top on artistic impression.

Getting time management right is at the root of achievement for those who can take the lead in several areas in life. Seb Coe – Olympic champion, successful businessman and now budding politician: Mary Peters – Olympic champion, businesswoman, team manager and outstanding community leader: Gerhard Berger – Formula One elite driver, businessman and now jet pilot: Katarina Witt – Olympic champion, businesswoman and now a sophisticated entertainer: these are all people who took the lead in one field and are still taking it in whatever they set their minds to.

People who take the lead, mountain people like you, work on their personal approach to time management and then weave into the framework of their personal preparation plan the other control skills. These, I believe come under two broad headings: the people business and the thinking business.

The people business

Communication skills are required in every occupation in some shape or form. They are fundamental to someone whose function in a business is communication. They also, however, represent the very lifeblood of modern dynamic businesses. How many organisations do you know who have hit a situation where they could say with the same feeling as Paul Newman in his role as Cool Hand Luke, 'What we have here is a failure to communicate.'

They include the requirement to write and to speak clearly and succinctly, whilst being prepared to listen and to respond. They also include effective and efficient use of the rapidly changing world of communication technology. In any business going through the culture change of a more open approach to communication, they must also include the ability to communicate across professional, management and departmental boundaries.

James Thurber certainly did not understate the situation in commenting: 'Precision of communication is important, more important than ever, in our era of hair-trigger balances, when a false or misunderstood word may create as much disaster as a sudden thoughtless act.'

The ability to communicate is, quite wrongly, assumed by most people. In my opinion, it is this assumption which causes most hiccoughs in any aspect of our life. You see, it is one thing saying, we must communicate more – it's quite another being able to do so.

Tom McKean, gold medalist in the 800 metres in the 1990 European Championships, was an above average club athlete coming into the 1985 season. In a period of five weeks in 1985, he went from being a labourer in Lanarkshire, Scotland, to being European Cup 800 metres winner in Moscow – and talking in TV interviews to millions of people. The difference in the requirement for communications skills was large. He was from then onwards expected to have opinions about all sorts of things and to be able to communicate them. Communication skills have their place, then, in every personal preparation plan.

A common language is obviously the first criteria we need for communication. As our integration into a pan-European culture advances, we will need to learn new

People stay hungrier and sharper
if you can give them what they need
not necessarily what they want.

(page 128)

language skills, but you'd be amazed how often two people can find themselves speaking the same tongue but lacking a common language. In my own experience I know that there are quite a few shades of difference between the language of the track-side and that of the board room. My coaching work makes me particularly sensitive to this because I work with successive generations of young people. But it is also true that among the experts I work with the technical language of coaching has developed rapidly over the last few years. Personally, I'm quite happy to engage in a banter which lets people laugh at my attempts to keep up to date if it encourages them to meet me half-way. Certainly, I'm convinced the burden is on the coach to try and bridge whatever gap there may be. If you've got something to say it's your job to put it across – you can't necessarily expect the other person to try and understand you. This is like the reception British businessmen first found in Japan when they assumed they could sell in English. The polite reply was that while the Japanese did everything in their power to sell to us in English, when we were in their country they expected us to talk to them in a language they understood. Often the only effort required is to learn a few phrases in another language. You may not be able to say much, but you will have communicated one clear message – that is, good will on your part.

In the late 1980's and early 1990's, several businesses shifted from public ownership to privatisation. These businesses went through a time-warp of culture change. One day there was the complacent security of no real competition and of passing responsibility for decisions up the bureaucratic ladder, the next there was the excitement of challenge and accountability which comes with competition and with having to be responsible for decisions. Most businesses communicated the nature and implications of these changes to everyone but very few focussed on the most basic requirement implied by the change. That requirement was and is for people to communicate in a different way than before and better than before. Everyone in any business should consider review and development of communication skills every year.

Membership of the European Community certainly suggests that we should each equip ourselves with communication capacity in at least one other language. Technology's accelerating revolution suggests that we are regularly retrained in how to apply its incredible potential to our advantage. Just think what mobile telephones, faxes, and electronic mail systems have done already to equip us to communicate and make decisions. Just think how quickly communications can shift your focus of resources from the content of your filing cabinet to a global perspective.

Working to improve communication skills at a general level extends its benefit well beyond occupation. There can be few families who have escaped the odd misunderstanding due to a communication problem. At a personal level, my communication nightmares range from being completely out of synch with the lastest additions to the English language picked up by my daughters in the school playground or from favoured

TV programmes, through to coping with my wife's incredibly sophisticated sense of timing in discussing a credit card bill.

People orientation requirements are tightly bound to communication skills, but extend their application. Whether it's being part of an Olympic team and living in an Olympic village, or being part of the love affair which exists between press/media, public and players in international tennis, athletes need skills in people orientation. By the same token, in many amateur sports, people are appointed as team managers but may not have the background which has required the exercise of people orientation skills. The situation is not dissimilar to that where someone's technical competence leads to his or her promotion to a management role where people orientation skills may have a higher priority than in his or her former position. They are a necessary aspect of personal development.

If communication skills are the life-blood of modern dynamic businesses, people orientation as a quality, is the muscle. Again, like communicating skills, you require this quality whatever your position in a company and, indeed, in life in general. None of us can achieve in life without relating to other people. Managers, sales personnel, people working within a team, human resources people, teachers, doctors, people in service based industry – all of us need some degree of people orientation. This quality is not something you have or learn through books and lectures, it develops through experience. It has to be practiced and worked at with new approaches hungrily pursued. This is where your sleeves are rolled up in the people business. It is about understanding the views and feelings of others and making them comfortable in expressing them to you. It is about being able to motivate. It's about being able to work within a team, and being committed to building it. It is, finally, about this very process we are discussing – the development of people and the sensitive application of evaluating procedures in preparing personal preparation plans.

Leadership completes the trio of people business skills and builds on communication skills and people orientation. 'Sound leadership equates with the ability to manage change,' according to John Adair. I would expand this by saying that leadership is the ability to guide people to achievement through skillful management of change in their development. It is also the ability to adopt a style of negotiation, persuasion or debate based on insight into the behaviour and potential of others. In my opinion, it is coaching at its very best. Dwight D. Eisenhower summed up this concept of leadership perfectly as, 'the ability to get a man to do what you want him to do, when you want it done, in a way you want it done, because he wants to do it.'

At first sight, there appears to be a straightforward sliding scale of leadership needs from the chairman to someone joining the company from school or university. I believe, however, that at all levels in a company or within the teams and departments that make up a company, it should be the objective to develop each person's leadership qualities. Understanding something goes hand in hand with putting it into practice.

Understanding what a company's leadership has in mind during this period of change is facilitated when everyone believes that he or she has some kind of leadership role to play in the change and believes that he or she is equipped to discharge it. Moreover, the moment that everyone thinks and behaves this way, the company has actually delivered on culture change in the process.

In sport, it is seldom that the best perfomer makes the best leader, captain, coach or manager. Leaders have the job of getting the best out of athletes individually and collectively. The best performer looks to being so. The roles, then, are different and the qualities required are also different. It could be argued that it's best not to dull the performer's edge and concentration with the broader responsibilities of leadership. I believe, however, that all performers should be encouraged to develop leadership skills through experience of various levels of leadership so that the concept of leadership is better understood and leaders are, on the one hand, better prepared for the task, and on the other are afforded more positive support. Everyone, then, from moment to moment in his or her life may be required to exercise leadership qualities in some shape or form.

People business qualities are required at varying levels according to your role in a company. Their development, however, must be worked on at all levels. I see it this way. People come through the door to work for a company because of their technical knowledge and abilities. They are promoted upstairs for their capacity to manage. But they hit the ceiling, jump out of the

*Achievement is a journey
without an ending and the
hardest part of planning for this
journey is how to arrive at one
destination and look forward
to the next.*

(page 100)

window or are shown the door again for shortage of people business skills.

The thinking business

Strategic planning starts, I guess, with what we are doing right now. Again you need some capacity in this direction at all levels in your occupation, from planning the future of your company through to planning your own life. Because every athlete should be involved in his or her own personal preparation plan design this must be part of development. Daley Thompson's involvement extended from four year planning right down to the monitoring which leads to weekly programme adjustments.

I think the starting point is effective and efficient time management. Klaus Moller, the founder of Time Manager International, pioneered pursuit of this starting point at a personal level but likened this to pursuit of a common system applied throughout a company. He also linked this to all three areas of the people business. I strongly subscribe to this concept and its variations as interpreted by other time management programmes. Consequently, I believe that time management is not more or less important according to position in a company. It is equally important – in fact, it is fundamental – for all of us.

It is also fundamental to be able to prioritise and structure objectives and tasks as a shopping list for action over anything from four to six years down to today, and when managing people to plan, recruit, coordinate and review their development and deployment, and the use of technical resources. This latter aspect does, then, depend on your role in a company, as does your requirement to assess tomorrow's trends in forward planning. 'You can plan the future by the past,' as Edmund Burke said, but you must also be able to visualise the world of tomorrow you're aiming for to design that plan. Rather more evenly spread, however, is the requirement to be able to create change, to respond positively to it and to manage it. Finally, it is also a more general requirement to relate your development and that of your team or department to the corporate planning for the company or even to business as a whole.

Decision making over the centuries is something that one small sector of any community has jealously defended as its right and the vast majority of the community have been advised that this is the way it is. The greatest single culture change in most businesses today compared with those of even the mid 1980's, has been encouragement of everyone in a business to make decisions and to accept responsibility for them. This, however, has required most fundamental changes in not only how we work but in how we think and relate to each other.

It has clearly been very difficult for people entrusted with this new level of responsibility to believe that they will be allowed to make and learn from mistakes, and that they will able to make the right decisions. The fact is, however, that this is the way forward, and people must be coached through this change.

I hold the view that the central aim of education is to prepare people to make correct decisions. In sport, it is only the athlete who decides on what to do in the arena. Preparation to do so runs as a most powerful thread through the training programme in practice. That preparation must give the athlete the basis for making decisions and the self-belief to do so.

Decision making, at whatever level, requires people to absorb information rapidly and analyse it objectively before reaching sound value judgements, making clear decisions or choosing action plans which are the most appropriate and effective. Decision making also moves people into the mountain territory of taking balanced risks and it is here that this culture change in companies has invaded the comfort zone of those who prefer the idea of letting others make the decisions and take the consequences. This really is a severe case of culture shock for those involved. I believe that this change in companies will continue, that it will benefit everyone concerned in their life in general as much as in their occupation, that it will be an uncomfortable learning experience, that we should all be coached through it and that it is right. Coaching will properly prepare us in the techniques of consultation when making decisions on problems whether they arise continuously or unexpectedly.

Complex analytical reasoning is something we normally associate with a company's strategic planning people and with those we've come to see as the decision making body, say the board of directors. I believe that the culture change which has cast a wider net for deci-

The deepest principle of human nature is the craving to be appreciated.

William James
(page 83)

sion making will lead to more people being involved in complex analytical reasoning and even more being developed to understand what's going on in this process. You see, nothing but good can come out of more people understanding the issues which are weighed in the scales of debate when a company's leadership must arrive at a best option action. People may not agree with the argument which wins through but they are enriched by understanding it. That enrichment on the one hand expands their personal knowledge, but it also expands their capacity to think as company people – as representatives of the badge and its values – as opposed to people who draw a wage or salary.

In arriving at decisions on preparation for an Olympic Games, a World Championships, and so on, I produce reports on each. These reports form the basis of the plan for the team and are produced eight to nine months before the games or championships. Each athlete who may be selected, the athlete's personal coaches and all team support staff receive copies and are invited to make comment before final decisions are made. In dealing with things this way, everyone is involved in the process of weighing issues and considering reasons for one action or another.

Clearly there will be people in a company whose occupation involves complex analytical reasoning as a main feature and many others whose occupations do not. We don't all have to be sophisticated in probing the facts and in assessing logically and critically but I'd like to know that there are people on my side who do so and

I'd like someone to explain to me in words that I can understand how it's done. Maybe then, I'll understand the comment made by a colleague when his company's Chief Accountant had recommended that the sponsorship of a local charity event be discontinued as part of a budget pruning exercise: 'The trouble with that guy is he knows the cost of everything and the value of nothing.'

Creative and lateral thinking is something we all need in abundance as mountain people, even if it is not considered a priority in our occupation. This said, it has become a feature of culture change in many companies that people are encouraged to exercise imagination and initiative. In fact, this comes in the same package as decision making.

Creativity is restricted by over centralisation,
too much decision making at the top, lack of planning,
empire building, and poor communications.

Anon

Thank goodness you and I have never come across companies like that! I guess that creative and lateral thinking is about giving your dreams a little more room to breathe. On the one hand it lets you understand the wider implications and possibilities of a course of action, on the other it exercises vision to see and create new opportunites to be innovative. The whole business of cross training where there is transfer of practice across sport has its origins in lateral thinking. Conditioning practices or athletic training have had a major impact in developing sport in general. New techniques such as the Fosbury Flop developed by Dick Fosbury in high jump revolutionised the event. This was some return for a small bit of creative thinking.

A coaching style of management

I have said that we all need to take the lead, to be coaches, at some time in our lives, as friends, parents and colleagues to one another. All these areas are important, but I believe there is one area where a coaching approach is often neglected but if applied could transform not only our personal lives but the economic life of our country. This is the area of management.

Every company in this country is presently experiencing culture change on a huge scale. Part of that change, I believe, must be a shift in management skills – leadership skills – towards those of coaching. These skills are necessary because every one of them is to do with people and preparing them to achieve more in their lives in general and, in particular, for the organisation to which they belong. This is nowhere truer than in the case of the one organisation we all belong to, Great Britain Plc. A country's greatest resource is its people and using them to their full should be any country's highest priority.

Many companies now recognise this need to use our human potential to the full and I fully support this greater application of coaching skills. Where I have trouble is with how the process of change is delivered in some companies and by some managers.

Yesterday's home runs don't win tomorrow's ball games.

Babe Ruth
(page 8)

The worst kind of hangover is the one suffered by winners who live on yesterday's triumphs.

(page 42)

It is not enough to coach an athlete by annoucing that you're going to do so with a fanfare and roll of drums, explain what you are going to do and then leave them to get on with it. You have to go through the process of personal preparation planning already described, updating that plan from time to time, and delivering on personal coaching for months, even years till the athlete wings his or her way into the arena. In other words, you stay with it as a coach, committing yourself to whatever it takes to prepare the athlete to achieve in that arena and the others that are to follow.

The greatest difficulties in developing and applying the skills discussed above arise where companies, themselves, and not just individuals within them have to be coached through culture changes. In these cases part of what management is changing to must actually be applied to effect the change.

Robert Horton, Chairman of BP, addressed such a need for culture change in an early speech to his staff. As he put it, 'Some leopards around here are going to have to change their spots... or I'll have to find other leopards.' The message was pretty clear. He knew that, as in every organisation, when change is announced, you get three kinds of response:

1. 'Let's go!' from those who see change as an exciting challenge that they may want to be involved in helping to shape. These are your achievers.

2. 'Let's see!' from those who may not feel competent to be involved in change or those who are yet to be convinced that the change will bring advantage. They are embryo achievers who need to identify change as challenge. The quicker they do so the quicker and more effective the change will be.
3. 'Let's quit!' from those who see change as too uncomfortable or even as a threat. These are your losers.

The clarity of Robert Horton's message would hopefully find the 'Let's quit!' group doing so quickly. The coaching approach which he was to lead in pursuing the process of culture change would turn the 'Let's see's' to 'Let's go's', and each 'Let's go!' to a 'Let's go farther!'

Because he needed to focus minds quickly and sharply on the seriousness of his commitment to change, and because he, of course, knew his people, I understand why he took such a tough initial position and admire the quality of the coaching approach he was to adopt in effecting that change. In a different culture, he might have taken a softer initial position: 'You've all been very successful leopards in the jungle. But the jungle's changing and even the best leopards are going to have to change their spots. I'm going to help you to do that. We're in this jungle together. But if this isn't well on its way to working by this time next year, I'll have to go leopard spotting!'

Hard initial line or not, the massive organisation that is BP has, indeed, most effectively changed its culture to remain a world leader.

Horton's example shows that there are no hard and fast rules for coaching. A good part of your effectiveness as a coach must come down to knowing the people you work with and knowing yourself. Even if you have absorbed everything the manuals say, you must still add something personal to your coaching. After all, coaching as a business is all about people and personalities, and this goes for coaches in sport and business. If you have mastered this you are ready to apply your skills as a coach to the organisation you serve and to the badge you follow.

CHAPTER SEVEN

THE BADGE

It's a great feeling to watch your flag reaching the top of the winner's flagpole at a major championships. You feel proud that you belong to it; that it's yours. Its successes are being recognised and respected by the world at that moment and you know a special sense of privilege in being involved in that achievement. What the flag stands for has won, and you are part of it.

Each of us has our 'flag' to which we feel this allegiance. It's the badge that symbolises our organisation. We've gone through our life being dedicated to achievement for and through such a badge. Some of our badges must change as we grow, others we remain part of for life. There is our family, our school, our team, our company all of which we learn to identify with and all of which we feel proud to belong to. In each case we accept the responsibility for representing our badge with distinction, for living and sharing the values it stands for and most importantly we learn that loyalty to a badge works both ways. Your organisation today has a badge you should want to be part of for life. That badge needs you with your qualities and commitment to the organisation to achieve in its arena. You need that badge with its qualities and commitment to you to achieve in yours.

Every organisation which is successful today can only hope to remain a winner through to the twenty-first century by recognising the importance of this athlete-centred approach to the continuing strength of the badge. The movement towards such an approach demands a culture change in every company it effects. The specific changes required vary from organisation to organisation but most have in common four broad headings under which successful culture change is delivered.

It has become fashionable to use mnemonics to remind us of key words for these headings so I'll use mine. I believe that those organisations which are best prepared for culture change are those which pass the **ACID** test.

Accountability
Commitment
Integration
Dream

Accountability

Accountability refers to the process of preparing people to be accountable for making their own decisions and for the consequences of those decisions. This aspect of culture change is designed to break down old structures that encouraged paper passing and permission seeking in a world where decisions were someone else's problem.

'Don't talk about it – do it,' is one expression of this new outlook. 'It's not making mistakes that hurts; it's not

*You can't sweep people off
their feet if you can't be
swept off your own.*

Clarence Day
(page 90)

learning from them,' is another. These are fine words, but they're worth little if the coach has not prepared the athlete to deliver. Delegation does not mean abrogation. It means applying a counselling style of coaching. The personal preparation plan must have as its objective the acceptance of accountability. This means accepting that you are just as accountable for the decisions you don't want to take as for the ones you do. You are responsible for making decisions you intuitively know the answer to and those you have to work at. The pay-off is that as skills and capabilities develop, courage and confidence follows. This is the crucial stage and a good coach will stay with this until it's right, because it's on the back of accountability that initiative will ride.

Decision making is never easy if you're new to it. It takes nerve especially when you know that making the wrong decisions some of the time comes with the territory. The only useful attitude to this is best summed up in the words of the indomitable Katherine Hepburn: 'What the hell, you might be right, you might be wrong... but don't just avoid it.' In fact, it's not even possible to avoid decisions. Not taking any decision is a decision in itself and usually the wrong one! We're all in this decision making business together and owe it to ourselves to develop our skills in this area, so that we can continue to smile at Mark Twain's words: 'I must have a prodigious quantity of mind; it takes me as much as a week, sometimes, to make it up.'

Winners, in my experience accept responsibility for their own actions and hold themselves accountable for success or failure. They pursue achievement as if they were the chairman of their own company. They surround themselves with advisors and ensure that they have ready access to the resources they need, but they make the decisions. The 'statement' is theirs, and they have to be their own boss, answerable to the face that looks back at them from the mirror each morning. At this point the coach is no longer in the driving seat; the athlete is. This is where he belongs and you've done a good job as a coach if you've helped to put him there. You've made it possible for him to be a winner in his arena, because you are a winner in yours.

These kinds of changes are not easy to bring about in an individual let alone a huge organisation. For many of these what passes today for the status quo has itself been arrived at over many years. No culture change may be effected overnight. The whole organisation must be coached through it with practices inevitably shifting quicker than attitudes. This takes time, work and, most important of all, patience as things sometimes move forward quickly, sometimes slowly, sometimes not at all. Even if things seem to be going backwards it is important to keep faith with your coaching and be patient, always patient. I recall at the time of the 1989 European Cup just after the British track and field team had triumphed talking to a number of journalists. They were all looking for an angle on the story and as the team had never come close to winning before they kept asking what had made the difference in 1989. My reply was that 1989 was no different to other years in the 1980's. This still didn't satisfy them and they kept asking for a story so in the end I gave them the story of chinese bamboo. When you plant it nothing happens in the first year, nor in the second or the third or the fourth years. You don't even see a single green shoot. And yet in the fifth year, in a space of just six weeks, the bamboo will grow 90 feet high. The question is, did it grow 90 feet in six weeks or in five years?

Commitment

Commitment, part two of the ACID test, is facing up to the challenge of change, from the game we have to win, to the culture change itself. There are three types of commitment common to any successful organisation. The first is to **quality**.

It's a funny thing about life, if you refuse to accept anything but the very best you very often get it.
Somerset Maugham

Quality should be striven for at every level from what the organisation produces or provides, to the preparation and development of its people, and therefore to the badge itself. It's to do with pursuit of excellence. It's also to do with dedication to perfection and to what it takes to get it.

When I was at Loughborough College, each Thursday night through the winter, I ran a four mile time trial from my room, across campus, round a road circuit, returning across campus and back to my room. It took me around twenty five minutes. Each night, on my way out and on my way in, I passed a row of ten or twelve saplings where I would always hear another student grunting with the repeated effort of sprinting and side stepping the young trees. I could only just see him in the dark and I always felt it was a miracle that he could avoid colliding with any of those trees. Finally, one night I stopped to see who it was. I couldn't contain my curiosity. This guy had to be special for his dedication and for his skill. It was Gerald Davis. At college he wasn't an outstanding sprinter but his side step sent many faster players sprawling on the college rugby field. Gerald's ambition was to play for Wales. He worked this way twice a week, every week going for quicker and quicker side steps. He did play for Wales and his genius remains the benchmark of quality against which every rugby wing three-quarter is measured.

How do you know if you've achieved quality? Put it another way. You will always recognise its absence. The more you work at personal quality, the better equipped you are to read your own performance. When the Russian ballet dancer, Vaslav Nijinsky was arrested and confined for long periods in cramped conditions, he clearly could not exercise. He considered that after three days without practice he knew the difference in the quality of his movements. After three weeks the public would know the difference. At this level, you know that when best is what you want, good is not enough. Quality is something you jealously pursue and protect in its reflection of you and of your organisation.

I consider a bad bottle of Heineken an insult to me.
Freddy Heineken

The emphasis on quality comes back time and again to you and me. As athletes we are responsible for the quality in our own performance but as coaches we are judged by how well our athletes are prepared for high quality achievement in the arena.

The next type of commitment is to **productivity**. I consider this to mean consistently producing quality. Winning once is hard, but you know it's possible. Winning again is harder, but you know then you're a winner. Winning again and again is harder still, but now the world knows you're a champion. This is what makes it tough to stay at the top as an athlete or as a team in football or tennis or any other sport in which you have long seasons or a year round requirement to produce quality. It is also what makes it tough to be number one this year – and next – and the year after that. But that's what our organisations must aim for. Of course, the momentum of one week's or year's achievement helps you through the next. But the fact is that each new week, each new year finds us climbing a new mountain. Commitment, then, to productivity, must be built into your personal preparation plan. Time for regeneration and development is especially important so that personal quality can remain high whilst being expressed repeatedly.

Quality and productivity must be considered together. To produce quality once you develop the personal capacity to achieve. You can go on producing it but the highest

*You don't come into coaching
for a comfortable ride.
Nor do you come in to sit
in the best seat. Ego's have to
accept standing room only.*

(page 93)

*You should always begin your
coaching from a position of
strength. What's going right should
always be the starting point, not
what's going wrong.*

(page 88)

productivity will only come when you develop the same capacity in others, in your athletes and your teams. Only then will your organisation be able to produce quality repeatedly. The important thing is not to mistake productivity by itself for quality. There's no point producing twice as much, or twice as fast if what you're producing is not your best. As movie mogul Sam Goldwyn said, 'A wide screen just makes a bad film twice as bad.'

The third commitment is to **people**. Culture change, when all is said and done, is people change because the culture is the people. They and only they can achieve the quality and the productivity you are committed to. Commitment to this goal is always shown through coaching because it's coaching that will keep the change 'people-centred'. They must feel that they are involved in driving the change or at least providing the energy for it. It is this that makes people motivated to change and even excited by it. It is this that makes culture change an achievable objective. They should not feel that the breakers of change are going to crash over them and bowl them helplessly along. That's not a commitment to people orientated culture change, so it's bound for disaster.

But commitment to people is also to do with those for whom we're making a product or providing a service – the customer. This is more than giving the customer higher quality or more of it. It means working out what the customer really wants in the first place. You can't just talk about culture change that's people orientated and ignore the customer. Tom Purves, Managing Director of BMW UK, took this on board when leading a quality customer service programme. He referred to 'customer delight' and stressed the need to sensitively apply to customers the same people skills we apply as coaches to developing the athletes in our organisation. The symbol of his approach to culture change was the blue print of a boat. The 'hard skills', associated with our 'technical business', are the hull and the rudder giving direction and stability. But the 'soft skills', associated with our 'people business', are more than just the brasswork and paint-work. They also include the mast and sails that give us speed through the water. Both sets of skills are essential.

What he was getting at was that the customer takes for granted the quality of the product an organisation sells. What they really notice is the way the product is sold and the after-sales service; the manner in which they are treated and the climate the company creates. When you project the image of quality that you wish the customer to associate with the organisation and, therefore, with the badge, you have to make the customer feel that he or she is part of that quality. Customers support a brand like BMW in exactly the same way that fans support a sports team. And like the management of any good team the management of a successful company shows a commit-ment to its supporters, a commitment to its people.

Integration

Part three of the ACID test means team-work. At this level, we're talking one badge, one organisation, one team. Culture change, in this context is seen by Sean

Lance, Managing Director of Glaxo, 'as not just about knocking down towers, turrets and parapets, but actually getting rid of the walls' that have separated the departments and divisions in many large organisations. Like medieval cities, they have been so jealously 'protected' from each other that the quality of communication and cooperation simply was not possible. So the first move in creating the right environment to pursue culture change must be this demolition job.

This means that people can move from the tunnel vision world of 'I can't help you because it's not my department' to 'I don't know the answer but I know someone who does'. It also means that the energies, motivations and abilities of people are no longer tied to one department or desk. Rather, the rich resource potential they represent is mobilised to be expressed in any one of several teams involving people shifting back and forth across 'territorial boundaries'. It means that people are rewarded for sharing information and ideas to achieve an objective. On the one hand this gives project leaders access to people throughout the organisation when choosing their teams, and on the other it frees people to work on a greater selection of projects individually and in different teams. There can be little doubt that a variety of challenges keeps motivation high, by affording people increased opportunity for development and achievement. For most organisations this brings much more than culture change. It brings metamorphosis.

Dream

Dream, imagination, creativity, lateral thinking – call it what you will – gives meaning and purpose to the organisation. Just as coaching gives to the athlete roots to grow and wings to fly so also to the organisation. And for the organisation, vision is the wind beneath its wings. This is the final part of the ACID test. Whether buffeted by wind and rain, or bathed in sunlight, the badge of your organisation must continue to reflect the vision of its people. The badge, then, stands for that vision. Maybe this is what makes the moment special when your badge is on the victory rostrum and when your team walks tall into the arena. There's no mystery to it. Vision is not something that comes from another world. It doesn't pop out of a hat. It certainly isn't designed by a committee. It always comes from one person – you. In the words of Tom Purves, we must 'demystify vision'.

Ideas are always there but too often they don't get a chance to come out. 'We tried that before', 'Don't make waves', 'We don't work like that here'. These all too familiar sentiments are an expression of a deep lying suspicion of change in some long established organisations.

It is an unfortunate fact that management in some organisations has depended uptill now on control of territory and of the minds of those who work in that territory. This kind of manager operates more like a referee than a coach. This makes it heavy going for creativity. This aspect of culture change requires sensitive coaching of those who have been in control as much as those who have been kept under control. Those who are used to being in control see ideas as a threat to what they understand as order. Those who have been controlled see creativity as undesirable conduct. When the rules change so that you no longer get a yellow card for an idea, players don't change their behaviour as quickly as the rules. I don't know too many people who can produce ideas to order especially when it has not been part of their previous game plan. Likewise, I don't know too many referees who actively encourage what they previously discouraged and even penalised. The 'referee' and the 'players' both need coaching through this change.

Ideas decide their moment, but this aspect of culture change will make these moments more of a habit and help people to recognise, in the words of Frank Capra, that 'hunches are creativity trying to tell us something.' It's that behaviour running through an organisation which is the seed bed of vision. The best example of this I've ever heard is the story of a visit by Alexander the Great, head of one of the most successful 'organisations' in human history, to Diogenes. Alexander asked the great thinker to name anything – anything at all – that he needed, anything Alexander could do to help him. 'Only stand out of my light,' was Diogenes' simple reply. The best thing we can do to help our people develop their dreams is to stand out of their light.

But making dreams reality is not easy. You cannot get commitment to making a dream come true if people don't believe in the dream. They'll only believe in it if it's theirs in the first place, or if they understand that their

*Sound leadership equates with
the ability to manage change.*

John Adair
(page 167)

*It's a bad plan that admits
no modifications.*

Pubilius Syrus
(page 100)

involvement is the magic needed to make it come true. To get that belief you must coach people to have vision and to want to give that magic. With this kind of coaching you have to be able to listen to what you need to hear, rather than what you want to hear. You see, even the best of dreams requires the fine adjustment that comes from listening, to give it a sharpness of focus which people need to see the dream as shared. Belief and commitment will surely follow.

The ACID test of culture change reaffirms and projects the values which the badge of the organisation stands for, to people in the organisation, to the 'customers'; and, of course, to the opposition. It seems almost a contradiction in terms to consider pursuit of culture change as a reaffirmation of values but in a sense change to meet tomorrow's challenges is the only value worth holding on to. The very fact that an organisation continues to create and manage change is a statement that this is a value it holds highly and lives by. Such a stance signals a company's commitment to achievement and to preparing its people for achievement. It's this that adds respect to the pride you feel for the badge that you have the honour to call your own.

WARM DOWN

The competition is over. The result is on the score board. These points – that fight – all are history. There's nothing you can do to change them. You can only use them to do even better next time.

There's either a hand on your shoulder knocking you out with elation, or a voice in the distance fumbling for words of comfort. Win, lose or draw, it's in these moments that you need to be alone inside your head, to go through what you're going to do with this result and how best to use it for tomorrow. There will always be other mountains no matter how high you climb today, nor how tall you stand.

Whatever the situation, you know that you are accountable only to the face that looks back at you from the mirror each morning. That's the face that really knows what the score means. You see, that's the person who sets your standards, that's the person whose quality has or hasn't been delivered. In the end, it's all up to you. You dream your dreams and ask 'why not?' You prepare to make them real, you coach and are coached to deliver and you do deliver.

Of course, things can go wrong but they sometimes do when you take the risk of winning – it comes with the territory. You know that's the case and you've learned to bounce back, because the truth is, if you can't take it – you won't make it. At worst you'll get criticism from a few of those valley people. You know what kind of criticism I'm talking about. It's like a 'professional foul' in a game of soccer, where someone goes for the player and not for the ball. It's my guess it's the offspring of jealousy. It hurts because it's become personal, but you've got to learn not to hurt, or at least not to show it. When that sort of criticism happens there are a few lines from a really great 'coach', Theodore Roosevelt, which I like to think about and I recommend you to do the same:

'It's not the critic who counts, not the man who points out where the strong man stumbled, or where the doer of deeds could have done better. The credit belongs to the man who's actually in the arena, whose face is marred by dust and sweat and blood, who strives valiantly, who errs and comes short again and again, who knows the great enthusiasms, the great devotions and spends himself in a worthwhile cause, who, at the best, knows in the end the triumphs of high achievement, and who, at the worst, if he fails at least fails whilst daring greatly, so that his place shall never be with those cold and timid souls who know neither defeat nor victory.'

This book has been written for mountain people – like you. I wish you all the success you deserve, not only in climbing your next mountain but in climbing all the mountain ranges where your ambitions and dreams will surely take you.